RESPECT THE WEEDS

Digital Transformation Rooted in Principled Leadership, Vision, and Innovation

BY ADAN K. POPE AND PETER J. BUONFIGLIO

RESPECT THE WEEDS
Digital Transformation Rooted in Principled Leadership, Vision, and Innovation
By ADAN K. POPE and PETER J. BUONFIGLIO
1. BUS071000 2. BUS070030 3. BUS042000
ISBN: 978-1-949642-53-7
EBOOK: 978-1-949642-54-4

Cover design by LEWIS AGRELL and JOSIE DIAZ-POPE

Printed in the United States of America

Authority Publishing
11230 Gold Express Dr. #310-413
Gold River, CA 95670
800-877-1097
www.AuthorityPublishing.com

For our daughters.
When they one day rewrite the book on leadership,
may their words be heard.

To Smita,
Thank you for teaching me
to ask the most powerful
strategy question:
" ... which means that ... "

Best,
Peter B.

CONTENTS

PART II: CREATING A UNIQUE POINT OF VIEW AS A FOUNDATION FOR CHANGE

PART III: PUTTING THE PLAN INTO ACTION

PREFACE

Weeds, as a type, are mobile, prolific, genetically diverse. They're unfussy about where they live, adapt quickly to environmental stress, use multiple strategies for getting their own way. It's curious that it took us so long to realize that the species they most resemble is us.

—British nature writer Richard Mabey, from
Weeds: In Defense of Nature's Most Unloved Plants[1]

You've been at this leadership game for a long time. You're good at it. Some days are great, some filled with anxiety, some are spent staring out the window of the platinum member airport lounge wondering what it's all about. What will be your mark on the world? Then you remember how you got here. All the people who depend on your leadership to keep the company lights on and the paychecks coming. Your staff hopefully admires you. That newly minted MBA thinks you're a walking Harvard Business Review case on mastering the art of reorganization, and the sales teams demand that your administrative assistant block time on your calendar for every prospective customer demo day. Yeah, life is good. Life was good.

---

[1]   Richard Mabey, *Weeds: In Defense of Nature's Most Unloved Plants* (New York, New York, HarperCollins, 2010)

Until that first-quarter strategy retreat.

Your business model has been upended. You're going to need to become a software-driven enterprise. To get there, you're going to lead a four-year, hundred-million-dollar "digital transformation" program to bring delight to the customer experience. And HR has been told that everyone in the organization—everyone—will learn how to code and focus on automation. Everyone is now a software engineer. This may sound strange to some, but the day of the citizen technologist is here.

You may know little to nothing about managing software engineers, software projects, software vendors, software integration, or software as a service. Even if you do and have managed the complexities of delivering and maintaining your current applications for a long time…well, those times are changing. Cloud, SaaS, disruptive business models, and changing workforce dynamics have all served to put pressure on your current business.

Take heart though, because you do know business. You know *your* business. It's changing, yes, but it's still your life's work and no startup or webscale giant can take that away from you. You know that mediocrity can never be tolerated, and you know that inefficiencies lead to disruption. And you know yourself. And you know that you're willing to learn.

All we ask is that you keep an open mind as we take you on our journey into digital transformation. We hope to show you the "other side of the test," the playbook from a competitor, or at least some real-world insight from the disruptive technologist perspective.

We know software engineering. We know software engineers. We know digital transformation. Both its power and its suffocating effects. We know software can be a dirty, ugly, gut-wrenching business. But we also know that software can bring big data, agile processes, bleeding-edge technology, lights-out automation, ideation, and innovation all to life.

This book presents a new perspective on agile leadership principles, from presenting vision and authenticity to building trust and creativity and positivity geared toward: (1) a digital workforce that grew up in a cloud-based, crowd-sourced, work-life balancing act; (2) the traditional systems engineers who already have answers to the problems that you haven't even posed to them; (3) the other leaders in your organization who will drag you into cross-functional KPI setting; and (4) IT consultants with pre-ordained technology solutions, abstract of any clear strategy setting.

We will then attempt to demonstrate how these agile leadership principles can be applied, particularly in how you look at making judgments, across the business, technology, and people domains. The software game is filled with imprecision, moving targets, competing interests, security threats, and the inevitable, sometimes inexplicable setbacks and failures that serve to have every decision you make ripe for scrutiny, or perhaps utter disdain. We will look at how deep thinking can mitigate organizational doubt with strong vision-setting, well-researched industry points of view, and stake-in-the-ground portfolio innovation and execution.

Putting these principles to work is the ultimate goal of this book. More than preaching theory, we hope to impart the courage to try these principles in your own organization, by describing case studies where they have been successfully applied, and also by developing potential use cases that your organization might face, in light of current digital transformation strategies and connective technologies emerging across market sectors.

Lastly, we know that good leaders need to challenge themselves, personally—to *dig deep*, if you will. At some point, you need to have the conviction to set and stick to your plan. To know when to challenge the dogma, resolve conflicts, and when to just let it go. And to take comfort that you're not alone. Your friends on the golf course are all facing similar challenges—whether it's someone in automotive manufacturing who needs to see a car as a hundred million lines of code on four wheels; or a retailer who needs to find a way to make shopping as rewarding as clicking; or the cable company that doesn't understand why millennials don't want to "subscribe" to anything.

This book will help you face the angst of digital transformation, with the courage to get out of your comfort zones. Close the laptop. Pick up a dry erase marker. Manage by walking around. Compete. **Respect the weeds that find a way to survive.**

PART I

DIGITAL TRANSFORMATION AS A GAME CHANGER AND A TEST OF LEADERSHIP

1

WEEDS PLANT THEIR ROOTS DEEP

The wave of *Digital Transformation* washing over the business world has inspired many headlines: a game-changer, a bridge between business and technology, self-disruptive, a fundamental impact on delivering value, and…as well…a buzzword, a balancing act, a double-edged sword, an exercise in lowered expectations, and a complexity nightmare. The desire to engage with a customer base that is more digitally savvy and whose expectations change with the social winds is pushing organizations to take a hard look at their outdated business models, processes, and systems. Leadership teams across the globe are trying to figure out how to take full advantage of emerging digital technologies—5G connected devices, the Internet-of-Things, cloud computing, big data analytics, artificial intelligence, and blockchain—to enable a fundamental reimagination of the value they wish to offer their customer and how to deliver it effectively.

If a digital transformation project hasn't landed on your doorstep yet, it will. If your current transformation project has turned into a cost-cutting exercise under the guise of improving the customer experience, you're not alone. If you feel like the business case for digital transformation isn't yet fully baked as the deliverables vary greatly depending on which department you are talking to, then tell your spouse that you're gonna be late for dinner—for the next four years!

If you already have transformation fatigue, don't despair—fortunately, this is not a book solely about digital transformation. This is, however, a book about coping with the taxing nature of transformation—on organizations, on innovation, on leadership—and how to stay on a path toward your desired business outcomes. Digital transformation *can be* the rallying cry to rethink your business and models, to reinvent the way you create value for your company, customers, and partners, and to revitalize the way you look at leadership and yourself as a leader. It can bring out the best in you, and it can pull the rug out from under your very best intentions.

Years ago, I was pitching a software system to the CIO of a well-known telecommunications company. The CIO, "Harry," was evaluating proposals for a hotly contested support systems transformation project. Transformation programs then, as now, were viewed as game changers: clean up the "spaghetti code" of bespoke systems that had proliferated over the years—a new service or technology historically meant a new system and new code. The independent software vendor that I represented at the time, as their CTO, put forth a value proposition to dramatically increase the level of data integrity while introducing unprecedented levels of business process automation. The anticipated outcome was that through sweeping systems modernization, our customer could create new services more rapidly, driving new revenues more quickly, while lowering labor costs through a greater degree of automation.

I believe that what Harry was struggling with was an uphill battle of corporate pressures, including a hypercompetitive market that rushed rollouts of broadband-hungry services, a tightening noose of regulations, margin pressures from declining legacy services, and a risk-averse portfolio strategy that refused to take the multi-service-play plunge into high-growth mobile communications. This better-faster-cheaper edict left Harry vulnerable to slick vendor sales pitches that promised career-ladder-climbing improvements.

Two years prior to our meeting, Harry had grown tired of his legacy operations software solutions provider, swapping them out for a nimbler and more fervent vendor. Or so he thought. After years of implementation that included an optimistic project launch, Harry's new system was quickly becoming completely unworkable and a complete loss for his company and his IT team. Fortunately for Harry, his executive leadership team recognized the complexity of the undertaking and put the blame on the vendor, not on Harry or his team. Harry's reputation for persistence and focus on delivery would carry the program onward, even in the face of a failed first attempt.

So, my team was pitching head to head with the original, legacy provider, who was now feeling vindicated that the free-wheeling replacement approach had fallen on its face. Harry was determined to get his operations modernization vision back on track. He decided that he would ask both vendors, the legacy provider and my company, to sit across the table from each other in a head-to-head faceoff. We were asked to make our pitches, and he and his team would pick the winning bid *by day's end*. I never saw a customer do this before, but this project had clearly jumped a few levels in the high-risk, high-reward game.

The faceoff started, with Harry at the head of the table and in complete control of this session. He laid out the ground rules and set expectations for both companies' representatives. We were given two hours to present our approach and offer in full—two hours to present a comprehensive, do-or-die story. Each vendor would then take questions from both Harry's team and the competition for an hour. There would be a short break, grab some food, and then the other party would repeat the process. At the end of the day, Harry and his team would dismiss us all, convene in private, and decide who they would trust to take on the project. What an action-packed day this was going to be, to say the least. Transformative.

Harry asked which company would like to start and I spoke up and enthusiastically volunteered to go first. After all, I was confident in our shared vision for the industry, the applicability of our technology, and the outcomes that we could deliver. My two hours went by quickly, and the questions were rolling in throughout the entire process, instead of being taken at the end as agreed. I really did not care because we wanted to show our confidence and the technical superiority of our solution.

Now it was the legacy vendor's turn. Their presenter stood up and said that the last two hours of my presentation was a clear demonstration that we didn't understand the complexity of the transformation at hand and that they could not do justice to such a complex program by trying to explain a solution in just two hours. Then they sat down.

I thought I had blown my chess strategy by exposing my queen so early. My teammates were rightfully annoyed at the gall of the legacy vendor. Our solution would not be ready on Day 1 and would require development over time. I knew it, the competition knew it, and we made sure Harry knew it. But, for better or worse, by that point, Harry had given up on vision statements and mindshare and was looking for the quickest route to cost reductions as the way to lead the industry. My team's "get it done" proposal won the day, won the bid, but ultimately didn't save Harry, as I had intended. His fate was sealed before the project got off the ground, as Harry was not working in an organization with a clear vision for their transformation, and everyone on Harry's team knew it. The world around them had changed, and resystemization was not a panacea for keeping pace with the industry.

Over the next decade, my company was bought out by a bigger solutions provider. I left the company. Harry's company was also acquired. He lost his office in the C-suite. The company that bought them out was also then acquired. Given the lack of clear strategy, all the restructuring and the moving business targets, the solution I had helped to design and sell was successfully deployed but failed to deliver the transformative results that we all had desired.

Years later, I had occasion to call on Harry once again. His small office was now modest and stark, and the once-bustling hallways were noticeably quiet. The air was thick with transformation disillusionment juxtaposed by motivational posters on the walls meant somehow to offer inspiration. One was an image of a basketball icon, Michael Jordan, extolling his winning philosophy:

> I'VE MISSED MORE THAN **9,000** SHOTS IN MY CAREER. I'VE LOST ALMOST **300** GAMES. **26** TIMES I'VE BEEN TRUSTED TO TAKE THE GAME WINNING SHOT AND MISSED. I'VE FAILED OVER AND OVER AGAIN IN MY LIFE. AND THAT IS WHY I SUCCEED.[2]

The only other piece of artwork on display was the iconic "Hang in There, Baby!" poster—you know, the desperate-looking cat dangling from a rope—that print that your kids hung in their rooms to help them survive puberty.[3] As I stared at that poster, I recall thinking, that our efforts to master transformation can't end like this. They just can't.

Before we leave Harry and this story, please know that he was and is an amazing technology leader and the story here is only shared to illustrate that even the most talented and well-intentioned amongst us may well stumble on the transformation obstacles that line their journey. We have nothing but admiration and empathy for Harry in this story. This is indeed the story of many more failed transformations than you may want to believe. It may be said that transformation derails more IT leaders' careers than it makes. Harry ultimately went on to

---

[2] From *Failure*, 1997 television advertisement by Nike, Inc.

[3] Original artwork published in 1971 by Victor Baldwin, adapted from *The Outcast Kitten*, story and photos by Jeanne and Victor Baldwin (San Carlos, California: Golden Gate Junior Books, 1970)

become even more successful and we all learned some valuable lessons from the experience.

We wanted to write this book because we felt that we are leaving a wonderfully flawed world to the care of a generation of leaders who may not have had the same access to mentors that we had. We wanted to write this book for those who have followed, challenged, contributed to, and sometimes pushed back on our leadership for many years, in good and bad, boom and bust, and who are now struggling to find a meaningful path in a world where experience is all too often neither recognized nor valued.

It has been said that authenticity
is the courage to be yourself.

A digitally-savvy, digitally native consumer base and workforce can see right through phony claims and ill-conceived leadership campaigns. Tell your kids there is a monster under their bed that will eat them if they get out of bed in the middle of the night and they will undermine your fable with a quick Google search. Tell your customers they can interact with you "digitally" through a chatbot and see how quickly they churn to a competitor after you provide them two canned answers, both of which involve rebooting. The double-edged sword of digital transformation might be that it brings your customer closer to your processes, but once inside your digital borders, they can see more of what really goes on in your operation. It's harder to hide. They will judge you on the *why's* more than the what's (watch any webscale company that was roped into giving regulator testimony in front of C-SPAN cameras). Both your customers and your teams will seek out and pledge loyalty to those they deem authentic.

I have often read that authenticity is the courage to be yourself, to which I would agree if we were allowed to add *based on a set of principles that you know to be true*. We set out in these pages to articulate a set of management principles that we feel will project the authenticity required to successfully lead organizations through the ambiguities of digital transformation. Our inspiration, and our unique perspective herein, are rooted in a steadfast approbation of courage. People are naturally attracted to acts of courage, large and small—from the feats of Navy Seals and first responders, to your child taking the training wheels off their first bike or standing up to a bully on the playground. For us, the ability to "be yourself" started from humble beginnings.

* * *

Before we proceed further, we would like to make a special request to our readers to aim to apply our stories to your life story and experiences. Our anecdotes shared herein will reflect our experiences: we will draw observations from the male-dominated sports in which we participated, and share accounts of customer meetings where leadership positions, particularly CIOs in the information technology industry, were predominantly filled by men. We can't change that. We considered trying to "Benetton" our stories, but, as you will see, we value authenticity to such an extent that we risk offending some readers rather than modifying observations to the point where they no longer ring true, undermining the very leadership principles we espouse.

We will try to convey in this text that we in no way view our recommendations as prescriptive, but rather inspirational, as we realize fully that the challenges that leaders face are unique to their organization, culture, and market landscape. Similarly, we can't begin to know the frames of reference of each of our readers—where you came from, where you are going, and the obstacles you face in getting there—so we respectfully ask your indulgence to abstract our anecdotes and apply them to your personal challenges and goals where they may fit.

To that point, while our experiences described herein reflect our careers in information and communications technologies, we believe that our learnings are applicable across market segments, with a little creativity from our readers. Our customers' customers spanned most commercial and industrial sectors. We saw many examples of enterprises where digital transformation offered eye-opening opportunities for organic growth and improved performance: from a mining organization struggling to turn over maintenance schedules to artificial intelligence platforms to an academic institution trying to retrain its faculty to use big data analytics to revise its coursework and catalog.

* * *

EVERY TUB ON ITS OWN BOTTOM

I have long thought of myself in the early years as a weed. Yes, the kind of plant that will struggle and grow wherever it lands. While I certainly don't want any more weeds in my yard, you have to respect them. They survive and even thrive where many a flower or blade of grass have perished.

I began life in what should have been a tranquil, solid lower-middle-class family in Indiana. I had very loving grand-parents, a devoted and fierce mother, an uncle who was a WWII Navy veteran, and decided to just be an uncle to my brothers and me, and I had a very dark, dishonest, and brooding father who was also clearly addicted to prescription medications. No, unfortunately, I was just not going to have an idyllic childhood. By the age of seven, I would be relocated to Ohio and experience a life dominated by the constant moving of our family, encoun-ters with many unsavory characters brought into our lives by my father, hunger, poverty, eviction, and ultimately the divorce of my parents. *No help was on its way.*

While the divorce turned out to be a blessing, the chaos of the years leading up to it left me forever changed and focused on making my life better. I'm reminded of *The Pilgrim's Progress,* a seventeenth-century novel by English writer John Bunyan, which tells the story of a good man's pilgrimage through life and an allegory to Christian perseverance.[4] Amongst his references

---

4   John Bunyan [1628-1688] *The Pilgrim's Progress* (Franklin Center, Pennsylvania, Franklin Library, 1981)

to endurance through self-sufficiency (i.e., no help on its way), Bunyan referred to the notion of "every tub on its own bottom"—of people taking responsibility for themselves.

While in elementary school, I had such an epiphany, in my own childlike way. In the midst of failing the third grade, I wrote a poem that would set the direction for the rest of my life: "*It's time to be a man and have a plan...*," I wrote. Not as eloquent as Bunyan perhaps, but for me, to this day, the idea of having a plan is on the top of my mind every time I undertake a new challenge. That desire to gain some sense of control and self-determination has been a fuel for my success in business and technology.

I started my journey toward a professional career like many young aspiring students. I worked hard in college to earn top grades, worked all sorts of college jobs to pay for my living expenses, switched to night school so I could earn more money, and ultimately graduated at the top of my class. I had a plan... and that plan was based on a basic, but easy-to-follow principle: "Do what ya got to do and get stuff done!" My plan was going to be difficult, and for me, expensive. I needed to maximize my outcome through what I would tell people was my "delayed gratification" strategy. This strategy basically puts all available energy toward a future goal while avoiding anything too distracting in the current day. If there was a test at the same time that I was scheduled to work, I had to do both! Go to work, go to class, and study. No complaining, no excuses—this was just part of the price I needed to pay for the future I wanted.

But the added benefit of working all the college jobs was that I was exposed to some very real "weeds" who provided me excellent examples on how to apply the "Do It" principle that I had embraced so fundamentally. One such weed was a software guy I met while working on an industrial control system that was destined for a steel mill in Baltimore. The steel mill ran 24/7 and could never be shut down or allowed to cool. The processes required to stay online were hard, complex, and even a bit scary. The most mysterious part, though, was the software. The enterprise only employed one full-time software guy. He somehow kept the line running, without fail; without him, these machines would sit lifeless. He was revered as an industrial artist as much as a technologist. This guy was known to work the evening after all the ruckus of the day was long gone. He would open a bottle of wine, blast classical music, and dance with the machines we had built and wired. The next day the robots would be moving and doing work and he would stay for an hour of overlap time, conduct his show-and-tell, and get any needed feedback. He did what he had to do, and got stuff done.

After finishing the work in that inferno, I moved to Columbus, Ohio, to get my BSEET (Bachelor of Science in Electrical Engineering Technology) from DeVry University, and upon graduation took a software developer job with AT&T Bell Labs in Naperville, Illinois. While Bell Labs didn't see me as a weed, per se, they did appreciate the notion of growing roots, including a formal mentoring program and a series of classes that were meant to help recent college graduates become productive employees. At Bell Labs, you could express your inner weed by becoming the quintessential "Lab Rat."

Lab rat was a nine-to-five job. Nine p.m. to five a.m., that is. The labs were a very-well-funded environment, and highly utilized, so I would scrounge lab time whenever I could. On one such night, my lab partner, Joe, and I were struggling to stay awake, while pounding away on a difficult network simulation. It was dawn and Joe broke free for a meal and a nap, while I stayed behind in the lab to guard our masterpiece. As I wasn't a coffee drinker, my solution to my sleep deprivation would be to exercise. Jumping rope. No rope? No problem. I grabbed some nearby communication cables and started twirling away. Pretty ingenious. Do what you gotta do. That was until a group of Bell Lab executives walked right into the middle of my exercise routine! But instead of chastising me for improper use of company assets, they respected the weed in me—they recognized the hour and the commitment and turned a blind's eye to my, what could have been embarrassing, antics.

My Bell Labs experience provided a boost of courage to take career risks in hopes of being trusted to solve the most complex technology problems and ultimately ascending into a leadership role. I moved from Bell Labs down the road (literally) to Tellabs, where I met the company founder and an amazing entrepreneur named Mike Burke. Mike was the kind of guy who knew every employee by name. When he saw any of *his* team out for a Portillo's hot dog, a Chicago favorite, he would come over to say "Hi," pat you on the back, and buy you lunch. Mike was truly a leader and an overall great guy. I grew up a lot during my seven-year stint at Tellabs. I started as a Software Developer on the TITAN 5500 Digital cross-connect system, which, in its day, was essentially the circulatory system of the US telecoms networks. I got my MBA at night school during this time, graduated, moved into product management, and then ultimately became the head of the R&D group for all of Tellabs management systems.

Then, suddenly, my courage was tested. Tested under the fire of opportunity and adversity.

SWIMMING AWAY FROM SHORE

I left Tellabs to make my fortune in what later became known as the dotcom (".com") bubble. I decided to stake out my own patch of the gold rush and I left Tellabs to join a local lame-to-fame icon in the video gaming industry, Midway Games. This company had invented the two-person fighter game genre with the introduction of Mortal Kombat some years before. I joined them to help create the Network Products Division, where we were chartered with helping the company to increase sales of their games by introducing a tournament concept. The idea was that we would enable competition based on the scores of other linked players, and we would reward them with cash prizes. The goal was simple: to generate more quarters into the coin boxes on tournament games. We did it by creating a networked vision of several games, connecting the machines via dial-up networking from bars, pool halls, and other retail locations. As our bonuses were paid based on sales improvement, my team and I camped out in our offices, bars, and pool halls and experimented with how we might create a more addictive game experience (and that reason alone, of course). We were ultimately able to create a sticky user experience, introducing instant gratification rewards, ways to customize cars, leader boards, and a coupon dispenser for beer and other location-specific goodies. Though we had success moving the platform to the budding internet, and earning more quarters, like everything from the dotcom era, much of the hype was without meaning...without purpose.

"You cannot swim for new horizons until you have courage to lose sight of the shore."

— William Faulkner[5]

I moved on, taking my first CTO job at a venture-backed technology company located in the northern suburbs of Chicago. The company had some initial success but had failed to establish a scale business and value proposition. They really needed innovation and reinvention of the product portfolio. But equally important, they needed new energy and a new approach to understanding their customers' challenges and the value their technology solution could bring. I joined just after the board had changed out the former CEO, under a new CEO who had fundamentally rebuilt the leadership team. I took on the development team and everything technical in the company.

This C-suite position was humbling. Creating a vision, a point of view, and a plan of action was clearly needed here. I learned a valuable lesson right from the get-go: scrutinize the company finances thoroughly before you join! I had not realized

---

5   William Faulkner [1897-1962] *The Mansion* (New York, Random House, 1959)

that the company was almost out of money as I stepped foot in the place. Our CEO was well into the process of raising a new round of capital, but this wasn't discussed as part of the interview process, and I was too green to know to ask. I like to say of my first CTO job, *you can do everything right and still fail.* The telecom bubble formed and burst as we worked hard to grow the company throughout this period. Then came the 9/11 tragedy in 2001, which we experienced from our boardroom during a customer workshop, knowing that our world had changed, yet somewhat perplexed as to how the event would deepen the economic recession. Within a few years, we sold off the technology and essentially shut down the company.

From these beginnings, I moved further into the Independent Software Vendor (ISV) market in telecommunications operations support systems, first with Cramer Systems, a UK startup, and later for Telcordia Technologies. I'll discuss these experiences in detail in the Chapter 10 case studies, but for now, suffice it to say that the ISV space was a constant struggle to stay "I"— to stay independent. Massive scale, extreme competition, and systems integration (SI) gatekeepers all conspired to pressure these companies to seek shelter in the form of M&A (Mergers & Acquisitions). Cramer was sold to Amdocs, and Telcordia (which had its roots in Bell Labs) was kicked around the proverbial playground between Bell System ownership, SI ownership, VC ownership, and ultimately (as of this writing) purchased by the Stockholm-based, global networking powerhouse, Ericsson.

It was at Telcordia that I met Peter Buonfiglio, co-author of this book, and a dear colleague for many years now. Peter was a marketing director at Telcordia, but he wasn't like most marketing folks I had worked with. We talked not about press releases and advertising, but about value creation; we talked about hype cycles; we talked about the unspoken voice of the customer. Over time, I discovered that he was a management consultant masquerading as a marketing guy. And he had a story behind his story. Like me, he came from a humble background, a middle-income, small-town hero made good.

He also learned how to stand tall against adversity.

Peter had lost his first job before he even started. He was hired out of Harvard to work as a strategic analyst for the CEO of a Boston-based investment house. The man hand-picked three Harvard grads to work for him every year. Peter felt very fortunate, he said, to be one of them. He was even more fortunate that he was given the summer after graduation to travel and play, before starting work in September. With one problem: it was the summer of 1987, right before the stock market crash. Peter was vacationing with his girlfriend at the time, at her family cabin on Long Lake in the Adirondack Mountains of New York. No phone line. No television. Only the local newspaper. As a spoof, her father brought a copy of the *Wall Street Journal* on his visit from their home in Connecticut. He knew Peter was going to be a big investment banker, so he thought he might enjoy a dose of the real world. Peter read every article in that paper. Page after page. Until he got to the Money & Investing section. There it was. "Moseley Securities Files for Bankruptcy." Ugh. Peter was adrift in a sea of impending doom. Black Monday.

His first career change set him on a course to want to help companies find success and avoid failure, aka Management Consulting. His resume reads like a greyhound rescue brochure, working with and for startups, turnarounds, equity carve-outs, and my favorite, the seemingly overnight commercialization of Bellcore (Bell Communications Research, which was later renamed to Telcordia Technologies), from a research consortium to a software and services vendor that had to learn about productizing, marketing, and selling.

His proverbial thick skin and forest-for-the-trees approach to life served him well when he faced his ultimate test…cancer. Peter was a weed being doused in chemicals and fire on a daily basis. Surviving cancer put everything into perspective. He realized the value of something more valuable than profits: time. Peter described the struggle to live from one day to the next. One hour to the next. One minute to the next. Then, in recovery, from minute to minute, hour to hour, and finally day to day, until you see time as merely a means to create. Where creativity serves to unlock the finite nature of time.

Time is a tool of creativity. Creativity unlocks the finite nature of time.

So why are we telling you all this when you can find our career paths on LinkedIn? Simple: context and experience matter. Everyone has a story, and ours have forged us to be the leaders we are now. Tomorrow will likewise bring new lessons, as sure as yesterday has already done, but our principles remain.

THE VIEW FROM 30,000 FEET

For thirty-plus years now, I have had the unique privilege and opportunity to work for and with some of the world's most innovative and exciting technology companies. I have held leadership positions since the mid-1990s and have done so all from Chicago, Illinois. The main difference, and thus one of the inspirations for this book is that my leadership roles have been with many companies on several continents and I remained living in Chicago the entire time. Needless to say, I am an experienced traveler. But this book is not about navigating O'Hare or the many other international airports throughout the world. No, instead, I want to share my hard-learned perspective on leadership and the challenges and opportunities in today's interconnected business world. **The value of a leader today has a lot to do with their ability to balance hubris and humility**, to take strength from within, and the openness to adapt and to maximize the best from any and all sources available. This takes skill, hard work, and a lot of sensitivity coupled with a solid dose of common sense.

While I don't believe that the challenges I have faced are required in any way to motivate or create strong principles or great leaders, I have found it vitally important to have a plan and then to manage to it, change it, beat it up, and breathe life into it every day.

What is great leadership? I think we all know it when we see it. The challenge has been how to emulate a great leader. Many books have been written on leadership "styles," where, by definition, a style is a method or set of mannerisms, that to us is more of an observation of the end result of personal principles and experiences. That's very hard to recreate or emulate. Leadership is one of those intangible things that we all really respect, hopefully aspire to exhibit, but can't quite grasp fully. We all probably have many life stories, both past and present, where we find examples of a true lack of leadership in peers, leaders, or subordinates. Sadly, a lack of leadership is all too common in many teams or even across entire enterprises.

For me, leadership is something authentic and organic that just comes naturally to the individuals who display it so effortlessly. I think this comes from a number of characteristics that are really more about the *individual* and their application of a common set of principles than their particular business or technical skills. Of course, we expect that people who lead functions, departments, or even enterprises, have the requisite skills in their discipline from which they may perform their jobs and understand the work of their employees.

Unfortunately, I have examples where leaders did not have any real related skills in their functional area, but this has not been common in my experience. We will dig deeper into domain knowledge in the next chapter but having a depth of understanding for what you are managing is extremely important from my perspective. If you have an area of depth from which to draw upon, at a minimum, that leader is most likely more self-confident and informed.

There are many books written on leadership and our hope is not to write another one with the same platitudes here. We wanted to share a more practical view of leadership and stories about some of the individuals who have shaped our careers and also who have provided us lessons from which to form a unique leadership style. That said, I absolutely do not claim to be a perfect leader. I, like us all, are a work in progress. Our hope is that the reader will recognize some of the principal traits of great leadership, enjoy some of the stories, and hopefully take away some practical perspective that they may incorporate.

2

ENGINEERING A NEW
LEADERSHIP STYLE

S teven Covey wrote the seminal book *The 7 Habits of Highly Effective People* in 1989 and I was one of the first to read it.[6] This was just a great read and still filled with great advice and truths that are applicable today. His premise, to *begin with an end in mind,* is just plain sticky, as they say. It makes as much sense now as it did then. How can you accomplish anything of great complexity or value if you don't have an end-result, an outcome, in mind?

This idea comes from the assumption that the expected outcome to be obtained is known, which resonates with my belief that I am a person always looking to the future with a point of view and a plan. As for the generations after mine, we need to look at their life experience if we are to lead them.

MANAGING DIGITAL NATIVES

We've all read the analyses on millennials: they comprise the largest block of the workforce, they want to use social media

---

6   Stephen R. Covey [1932-2012], *The 7 Habits of Highly Effective People: Powerful Lessons in Personal Change* (25th Anniversary Edition, New York, Simon & Schuster, 2013)

at work, and they may want to come in late to work and to leave early. But that's just what we tell ourselves because we are challenged by them. They don't conform to our norms. So, our default is to put them in a bucket to be "managed." I'll file that under leadership laziness.

Millennials don't care about the 7 Habits.

Millennials are a generation of digital natives. They were raised in an Information Age steeped with boundless connectivity, data, devices, and mobility. They grew up with the assumption that if you want to know something—anything—you're just a click away. If you want to buy something, just order it; if you want to connect with a person, join one of a thousand social networks. They use technology in ways that my generation could not even imagine (that is, not in the way that it was *intended*). They hack, they mash-up, they ask for the APIs, they live in the Cloud. They share, they crowd-source, they don't care about ownership. They care about getting from one place to another, about transportation more than the unsustainable car in the garage. Millennials don't care about *the 7 Habits*. They care about outcomes.

And they challenge authority. Here's the scary part. (Not scary for them, but for leaders.) They challenge authority, not out of disrespect, but out of the knowledge that authority can often stand in the way of getting to the desired outcome. The phrase, "That's not the way it's done," is meaningless to them. It's just a roadblock. And maybe that's a good thing, as my generation appears to have all but given up on solving some of the persistent, intractable problems that millennials have embraced: climate, hunger, healthcare, equality. Generation-Z (born after 2000), just coming now into the workforce, will be even more technology-enabled: they disregard advertising, user manuals, mainstream media, and combustion engines.

But here's why you need to pay attention: millennials bring unfettered creativity to your team. Because they reject or ignore the constraints and limitations of what's come before them, they see most challenges as a clean sheet of paper. They assume that any data set that is desired can be found. They believe in accountability and progressing any meaningful cause or goal. And they all (or almost all), have an appreciation for or have done some type of configuration of software. They create value in their lives and differentiate themselves via software and applications. A washing machine is not just a utilitarian device intended to make the process of washing clothes efficient and effective, but a smart device participating in a sustainable ecosystem, enriching the connected life experience!

All that aside, here's why you might be tempted to dismiss their ideas or ways of working: their mindset of incrementalism (informal project planning based on small changes) belies decades of systems planning, where the concept of precisely specifying, planning, and then implementing a project does not come naturally or easily. It's no coincidence that in the age of agile development, iterative and transparent methodologies like Scrum and Kanban have become the norm.

This new workforce tends to blur the lines between office life and the rest of their day ("of course I should be able to use Snapchat throughout the day"), and they expect their workplace to behave in the same way their home and leisure life respond to their needs. They expect technology to work on their behalf, not to work for the sake of technology. The lack of interest in ownership relates not just to cars and power tools, but to individual rewards and to leadership roles. They don't need to demonstrate their commitment to the task through heroics or martyrdom.

This new workforce expects their workplace to behave.

When I was a newbie, my employers expected that I would go to any lengths necessary to complete the mission assigned. Whether I was volunteering to work weekends or sign up for the three a.m. lab time, those commitments were seen as the price you paid for the privilege of membership on a high-performance team. The horrible lab time was noticed and it was the topic of the break room commentary by teammates and managers alike. The lab rat who fell asleep at his desk after an all-nighter would awake to a note carefully taped on the back of his chair: "Don't wake the sleeping developer." This was a badge of honor, not humiliation.

Ironically, the communications technologies that I worked on as a developer have enabled the "work-life" balance that millennials have come to expect today. Information at your fingertips, on any device, in any place, at any time. Broadband communications are regarded now as a basic human right in many countries. VPNs (virtual private networks) allow secure access from the local coffee shop, and normal "working hours" are meaningless, particularly as crowd-sourced work spans numerous time zones. Universal communications tools such as Slack® or Microsoft® Teams serve to create a virtual water cooler and drive a continuous, daily dialog across distributed groups of people.[7]

All this flexibility can lead to chaos, but it also unlocks the much-desired technical creativity from highly motivated and energized teams. Incrementalism may be different, but it is by no means deficient.

As I matured as a technologist, I also separated myself from my leadership peers, by embracing the flexibility that technology offers: worrying less about conforming to office norms and more about performance. At one point, I worked with a leader who had obviously come from the Bell Labs, conformist environment. He was demanding, did not recognize the differences in working styles of the younger employees, and as such was very frustrated that people were not still at their desks at six p.m. each day. I was commuting via train and needed to leave the office by five p.m. or so most days, to make it home in time for supper. The entire team and I were in almost constant communications—weekends,

---

[7] Slack is a registered trademark of Slack Technologies, Inc.; Microsoft is a registered trademark of Microsoft Corporation

early in the day, late at nights—and we were all fully committed to achieving our project goals, and the team was performing at a very high level...but the office was dark by six p.m.

My takeaway from that experience was that maybe we need to add an eighth habit for highly effective digital natives: *recognize that your peers and employees may work differently, but it's not necessarily wrong or ineffective.* The cultural norms we create should be about efficacy, not control, and let the culture grow organically within those norms, not despite them.

Great ideas and contributions come from the organic opportunities that present themselves when we create an environment where our employees can truly balance their work and business lives. The servers that run your business will be undoubtedly upgraded in the evenings and weekends; bad actors will attack your business whenever they choose, and the next big idea may be born on the back of a Starbucks coffee cup. Flexibility and inclusion drive not only a better working culture but moreover a fuller and more creative employee who is more able and willing to have the challenges of the business on their minds as they live their lives. This small investment we make in supporting our teams pays off many times over in their commitment and focus.

All this talk of millennials and generational differences might easily be read as a simple espousal of stereotypes. That's not the intention. I see patterns in everything and everyone that surrounds me. For every pattern, there are differences and nuances. We are only calling out the larger shape of the millennial experiences and teams we have worked with and led. So, this is not meant to be a statement of value or social anthropology...just some (hopefully helpful) observations.

STANDING ON THE SHOULDERS OF GIANTS

So, if digital natives are the source of all things innovative today, then why are so many high-profile technology companies stumbling as they mature? The answer may lie in the nature of incrementalism: that while a lack of precision and planning structure is what allows for speed and agility to get a new idea to market, those strengths can turn into shortcomings when growth curves begin to fall back down to earth and stakeholders (including customers) start to open the hood of the car to see how the engine runs. Protecting privacy may not be an issue when you're signing up customers by the millions—and they "opt in" to your policies—but when your CEO gets dragged in front of Congress with only promises to investigate the loss of customer privacy, can cause a twenty percent stock price plunge when the market expects real process controls and authenticity. Apologies and promises fall far below the expectations of Sarbanes-Oxley controls.

Maybe to move forward, you also have to look back. Maybe those veteran employees who still want to read operating manuals and advocate for proprietary platforms, and who won't upgrade their operating system until the first set of patches are released, are also the same people who wrote code in the 1970s that is still running effectively at global telecommunications, banking, and airline companies. These are the people who pioneered five-nines (99.999%) reliability for those markets. You may have in your ranks today the technologists that have the foresight and holistic thinking to industrialize the new digital offering that you are trying to push out the door as quickly as possible. After all, we are standing on the shoulders of the information systems technologies that thought to digitalize our lives in the first place.

We are standing on the shoulders of the information systems technologies that thought to digitalize our lives in the first place.

Have you ever taken a moment in your day to marvel at the immense progress in technology we have all experienced in our lifetimes? My first experience with computer technology was during an electronics shop class in high school in the late 1980s. They had some old IBM data processing machines in the corner of the shop. I'm sure they had been donated, but no one really knew how to use them.

My brother went to college a few years ahead of me and he needed a computer to do the required schoolwork. The best computer at that time was the Apple IIe. He asked our grandfather if he could make the purchase for all of us. Our grandfather had grown up on a farm, taken a horse to school until he graduated, drove trucks, and ultimately retired after many years of work in an iron mill, so every dollar he had earned...he had *earned*. Within a generation, he was buying a personal computer for his grandsons. It was clear that I would be going to college as well, and that personal computers were going to be an important asset for anyone pursuing an engineering degree at least.

Compare that to today, where with the help of YouTube and some open source communities, you can develop an application for iOS that has the opportunity to reach a billion people, all from your corner Starbucks, with the aid of some their sweet free Wi-Fi and tasty brews.

We need to remember that we are at this point in history because of the work of many amazing philosophers, engineers, artists, scientists, and geeks!

Although we may consider many of these early technologies to be obsolete, there would be none of today's modern miracles of technology without these humble beginnings. And the beginnings did not feel very humble when they were new. In the same way that the webscale players feel less like they are developing a platform for twenty years from now, and more like they are turning the world inside out.

While the old guard can pass the tests of time, some may struggle now to understand their current role in this era of digital transformation. And we don't make it very clear for them. For every management fast-track we offer to a thirty-something up and comer, we offer little to none for the names on the "Celebrating Anniversary" slide at the end of the staff meeting. "Thirty years with the company? Wow, that's amazing. They could retire whenever they want."

They don't. They stayed for thirty years because they love the work. They love complex challenges that require even more complex solutions. They are engineers. They love engineering and reengineering things. They love the learning and sharing environment and meandering through offices with whiteboards filled from corner to corner, with bag lunch in hand.

What they may not be as comfortable with is simply how to take the *leap of faith* required from this new digital age... this digital *transformation* age. All their professional experience trained them that you didn't sit at the computer screen until you had <u>all</u> the requirements defined and architectural dependencies mapped out. You didn't approve Marketing to write the brochures until the product was "GA" (General Availability in the software release lifecycle); and Sales, well, if you even hint to Sales about anything new, they will immediately turn off the spigot on your legacy revenue streams.

Your job now is to formulate the best-of-both-worlds organization. Both of these mindsets, the old guard and the revolutionaries, have some common ground that you can leverage. They both value a vision for the future, and they both disdain mediocrity.

THE UNDAUNTED LEADER

It seems today that leaders all too often act as if the organization is all about them. While it is obviously true that the leader needs to lead and set the tone, the organization is about the purpose and vision and NOT the leader. The leader absolutely must express their highest aspirations of leadership each and every day and be the best example of the behaviors they want to see in their teams, but chief among those behaviors is humility and fairness. It is a massive mistake to lead from your ego.

We all have an ego. We all have our stories and experiences which have shaped us, but when we allow these experiences and our ego to define us and lead from this place, we fall short, and our teams will see through this façade.

Believe it or not, I have worked for leaders who referred to themselves in the third person. It's the kind of over-acting characterization that you only see on daytime television. In one such instance, the leader had decided to leave the big corporate world to take on a struggling, small private company. This person was really a very polished, skilled, and respected executive in the industry, in the classic realm of corporate leadership of a large diverse organization. He had worked his way up the corporate ladder all the way and then suddenly ended up at the head of a very small tech company. I am sure that this was a hard transition. He expressed many times that just because he was now the head of the smaller company, he would still remain true to himself as he had throughout his career.

In one such case, a colleague and I had been diligently working to engage practically the entire company to deliver on a very poorly written and open-ended contract which had been entered into by the prior regime of leaders. The contracting was legitimate, but the scope of work and definitions of success were simply undefined. After much-difficult negotiations and hard-fought progress, we had scoped the deliverables to a point where they had been achieved and were ready for acceptance. The one caveat was that the director-level project owner at the customer had demanded that our company head traveled with us to their headquarters to seal the final scope and make the final commitments before the final acceptance of the project. Our leader simply refused to meet this demand. This "director-level guy" was not his hierarchical peer, and that was the purpose of his staff anyway: to take care of these situations and commit and deliver for our customer. So, my colleague and I traveled to the customer knowing full well that we would disappoint our sponsor. Sure enough, the first question from our customer as he greeted us in the lobby was "Where are they?" We were sent back home with our tail between our legs and no sign-off or commitment for the final phase.

He was a truly honest and deeply thoughtful person and leader. However, the gap continued to widen as employees found it difficult to connect with him, as many of them had never worked with a person so senior. While he was open and transparent, he did not always appear to realize his audience just did not have the same perspective and context. How could they?

The highest expression of leadership is the servant leader.

From my perspective, the highest expression of leadership is the servant leader. This approach leaves the ego out of the mix in favor of coaching and collaboration. Surely there are many types of leadership and each leader has a different mix of skills and approaches to bring to the role: a leadership "mosaic," if you will. As for myself, I aim to start with this approach in mind and try to always use the words "work *with* you" instead of the more traditional "works *for* you." It's true that organizations are mostly hierarchical, where the chain of command and delegation of authority is clearly written on elaborate org charts. The people at the top of the chart are deemed the leaders and those below are workers. While there is an obvious need and value to a clear line of authority, the expression of this authority must not be our first or even top-ten choice in leading an organization. If you need to tell someone that they work for you and you expect that they perform a task, you have completely failed to lead. Instead of leading and coaching, the *dictating* approach has removed the ownership and empowerment from the individual and instead placed it completely on you as the leader. You may get a result, but more likely the team will provide nothing more than perfunctory obedience to your edict. If the task fails, it's the leader's fault, as they chose all aspects of the path to be taken. If the project succeeds, the team will likely not feel the sense of accomplishment, as they may have never felt the sense of ownership that comes from true collaboration and contribution.

I am not proposing that we shirk our responsibility or accountability as leaders. Instead, I am proposing that your best chance of creating the outcomes for which you are ultimately accountable is to take the approach to lead from the front instead of from the corner office. See yourself as a special member of the teams you lead instead of their boss or the executive. A simple way to express this approach in tangible action is to physically join a sample of the working meetings instead of getting the minutes.[8] No one expects an executive to sit in on every code review, but perhaps they should attend at least once in a while to really understand what the team does and how they go about doing it.

The closer the leader is to the function, I believe, the more familiar that leader is with that scope of work. If you take this approach, the team will recognize your involvement as leading from the front *with* them. A leader is far more likely to make informed decisions, as well, if they are armed with at least some degree of firsthand experience. See yourself as a coach, but not the kind that tears the team down. Be the kind of coach that is truly there to help the team achieve greatness. Be the kind of coach that will play the game with the team and who will jointly own the wins and losses. In this way, you will become less scary and more approachable as well. The team will reward the leader with honesty and their true intention to achieve the goals of the organization.

Sometimes a leader may appear to have all the right traits and skills on display to the people who report to them, while

---

[8] It is absolutely critical in these first-hand engagements that the leader does not take over the meeting. Let the team function as they would normally. Your goal is to learn and be informed and to join in the meeting or project. You are there to participate while you let your leaders in the team do what they do. This does not mean you should feel as if you cannot participate in these sessions. You absolutely should do so, but in a manner that is on the same level with the team. Ask questions instead of telling people what you want. This alone will go a long way in building trust and understanding. If you have made an individual accountable for leading a project, then direct any major course-changing feedback to them. Delegation of authority and accountability is only effective when supported by actions.

those who they work with outside their organization may have a completely different perspective. This duality exists within us but may be amplified in the business setting. Although we aim to maintain our principles in all that we do, it is all too easy to see internal organizations as competitors and as a result, devolve into an "us and them" culture. Earlier in my career, I led all the development groups within a software division of a large company. We were small, messy, very different, and always trying to sell the internal value of our applications to the broader company and our sales teams. Their behavior was more to give our applications away while they went about the "real" business at hand. Our top leader was really outstanding in many ways. He had a vision and we were all bought in, we had all collaborated on creating it and we all were true believers. This person was authentic, open, collaborative, and clear-minded. We all loved him. As it turns out though, the organizations of the larger company saw him as abrasive and difficult at times, and as a result, transferred much of their ill will onto all of us.

This behavior set up an environment of internal strife and competition which really did not help anyone achieve their objectives, let alone creating a toxic atmosphere with our colleagues. The point of this story is simple: all of your daily conduct and interactions reflect on the teams you lead. Take great care to express all those great leadership skills to not only your team but also to the entire company in which you reside.

We all have worked for leaders with temper issues; we all have felt unfairly held accountable for matters outside our control; and we all, likely after these experiences, have felt smaller and less engaged and less empowered as a direct result. I once took a job at a company where the executives were truly amazing during the interview process. I met with them all a number of times and felt secure to join the team as their CTO. I truly enjoyed our meetings and felt that we would work well together as my peers had solid business skills, were very articulate, and had a solid grasp on the industry and its competition. What they needed was a person like me to take over all the technology, as they had limited knowledge or patience for it. I thought…perfect!

Within six weeks, I was in my new office and getting up to speed when I called one of them to ask advice on how to begin to handle a strategic project that had been well underway before I joined. The matter had to do with the due diligence on a company that was under consideration by the board for acquisition. In my judgment at the time, I needed to bring another person in the team into the project and under the non-disclosure. I felt that I did not have enough context on our products and business yet to truly assess the strategic technology fit and integration issues. It just made sense to me. Instead of getting a simple approval—I got a threat. "You had better….," in an angry voice. Initially, I was shocked, but within an hour I was in this person's office; I decided to ask him exactly what they meant by "I had better." For that hour, I was readying myself to resign. The meeting with this person was strained to say the least, but they resolved to communicate in a more respectful and professional manner.

As the days turned to weeks, and weeks to months, my team became more and more comfortable with me as their leader. Many of them shared very hurtful stories they had experienced with the same leader. At times, his action made the team feel unvalued. He appeared, when frustrated, to lead from a place of ego and as a result, had created fear and uncertainty within the team. I spent a lot of energy and time with my team and with this leader. They received what they needed the most: confidence, collaboration, and support. As for myself, I developed a relationship with this person, too, but now based entirely on professionalism and very clear communication.

The Absence of Ego

We began this chapter with stories of humility. My experience with a leader struggling to understand why he could not get results from his staff—even after *telling them what to do*— wasn't just a serving of humble pie to someone who clearly deserved it, but a lesson for me as to how easy it can be to become blind to our ego. Leadership roles are typically bestowed upon the person who displays superior knowledge, judgment, and track records of success. They are also granted decision-making authority, financial controls, and sometimes corporate perks (in the Bell days, the size of your office was pegged to the number of staff you managed). It's understandable that a person's sense of self-importance could be tied to an inflated sense of being clever and correct as the reasons for being given, and maintaining, the role of leader. Being the leader can even become a major part of one's identity.

The rise of servant leadership could be viewed, in part, as a movement to combat ego in business. Servant leadership, where leaders put the needs of others before their own, was introduced in essays by Robert Greenleaf in the 1970s but became mainstream in Simon Sinek's 2014 book *Leaders Eat Last,* which put a spotlight on human interactions with a title inspired by the servant leadership in the United States Marine Corps. Sinek argued that "real leaders" in the military were born with those abilities instinctually, biologically.[9]

Servant leadership has served business well, particularly through times of great uncertainty. The pace of changing consumer demand, business model disruption, and political and economic apprehensions required organizational structures that could adapt and overcome market forces. In war, they say, strategy goes out the window once the first shot is fired (servant leadership is required for the troops to overcome the fog of war in real time). Servant leaders make sure their teams have the processes and tools to succeed and make sure their reports *know exactly what is expected of them.*

But servant leaders still need to draw upon some mix of insight and "gut" to set strategies, based on their best judgment, founded on their superior knowledge. That strategy setting cannot be swayed by a fear that their teams, to whom the leader is now subordinate by definition, might undermine the leader's objectives

---

[9]   Simon Sinek, *Leaders Eat Last: Why Some Teams Pull Together and Others Don't* (New York, New York, Portfolio/Penguin, 2014)

in pursuit of executing the strategy. A Marine captain can decide how to flank the enemy to take a hill but cannot question the orders of their leader whether or not to take the hill in the first place. The clear-eyed intention required to set the strategy becomes the same belief structure that must defend it as truth, attempting to take the fear and resistance out of the troops as well.

Knowing Exactly What Is Expected

The leadership "styles" that authors and consultants compare and contrast are mostly derivatives from a 1939 study by psychologist Kurt Lewin who observed three contrasting methods: (1) Authoritarian, (2) Democratic, and (3) Laissez-faire.[10] Each of these, and their modern forms, including servant, visionary, and player-coach leadership styles, was necessary for the place in time in which they thrive (e.g., autocratic leadership was required for manufacturing sectors where strategic objectives required efficiency and process adherence). In each of these styles, success seems to depend, to some significant extent, on the ability of the leader to convey exactly what was expected of themselves and their teams.

What we have observed, and a foundation for this book is that once inside the cloud (pun intended) of digital transformation, where technological change far outpaces organizational change, the lines of what is expected become blurry and incongruous. We don't believe that the current leadership styles hold when faced with such profound change. Marketing technology guru, Scott Brinker, described a conundrum that he posited would become the greatest management challenges of this century, which he

---

[10] "Patterns of Aggressive Behavior in Experimentally Created Social Climates," Kurt Lewin, Ronald Lippitt & Ralph K. White, *Bulletin of the Society for the Psychological Study of Social Issues*, 1939, Issue 10.

dubbed Martec's Law: "Technology changes exponentially, but organizations change logarithmically."[11]

"Technology changes exponentially, but organizations change logarithmically."

—Scott Brinker

Brinker was tracking the number of marketing software applications that were available to marketing professionals from year to year. That number grew from a few dozen to a few thousand in a handful of years. Overwhelming to say the least. A daunting task: to manage an organization whose ability to differentiate and compete may rest on the utilization of the best technologies to enhance the customer experience and interaction with the brand. Even a so-called visionary leader would have a hard time mustering enough trust from an organization mired in constant evaluation and fear of sub-optimization.

A Man Paints With His Brains and Not With His Hands

One obvious answer to combatting Martec's Law would be to try to change the shape of the curves to meet each other: engage a Pacesetter Leadership approach to drive changes more rapidly through an organization, whilst adopting Democratic Leadership elements to corral technology decision-making. But as Michelangelo was quoted as saying: "A man paints with his brains and not with his hands." Michelangelo wasn't just a painter and sculptor of the human form; he was a student of human anatomy. He wanted to know what was underneath the skin

---

[11] Scott Brinker, "Martec's Law: The Greatest Management Challenge of the 21st Century," *Chief Marketing Technology Blog*, November 6, 2016, https://chiefmartec.com/2016/11/martecs-law-great-management-challenge-21st-century/

and muscle tone so that he could better understand the how and why—reportedly going so far as to conduct dissections of the corpses that ended up at a local monastery when he was a teenager. Sculpting the human form in a convincing way was a daunting task. Michelangelo was an *undaunted* artist.

We believe this undaunted dimension of leadership is, at times, missing today. The Undaunted Leader, able to persevere through the potential chaos and debilitation of digital transformation, would then embrace these key characteristics:

o Bereft of ego and the need for accolades

o Knows that the answers exist somewhere in the market-place, in places that only a "weed" would find

o Rests assured that the principles abided are more important than the destination

The Undaunted Leader knows the challenges will be large, knows resistance will be high, is willing to do the work to form a point of view and to engage and develop their team. And they are not daunted by any and all of this because they know that by being undaunted, they will gain the support they need to achieve the results they will need to progress their digital transformation.

This is Not a Quest to Be Liked

Leaders are challenged every day to make hard choices, to take the hard road. To do what is right regardless of the decision's popularity. It is why they are respected and why they are often disliked. As a leader, which would you prefer if you could only choose one outcome: being liked and not making too many waves, getting along with your leadership peers and their organizations, but contributing incrementally and not fundamentally making a pivot for the business; OR, being as highly effective as you can be to steer your business to a future based on a breakthrough vision, driving the highest possible returns for yourself and your stakeholders? For me, the answer is simple: I want to be liked...I am human and have the same wants for social acceptance, friendship, and self-actualization at work as much as in my personal life. But—and this is a critical difference—I don't *need* to be liked to be effective. I measure my own contribution based on an effectiveness toward accomplishing the objectives of the business and its shareholders. I simply must put the objective ahead of my personal desire to be liked by everyone.

I realize that my CTO perch has afforded me a direct connection to the CEO and many times the board of directors, and that status may appear, to many, to offer inherent privileges of some sort. But I assure you that reporting to a CEO or president of a business is no safe place to be.

So, there is a clear choice in taking an *undaunted* approach. I am confident enough to know that if I'm driving the objectives of the company and the CEO, I'm most likely to find my best outcome and that of the company; I put my apprehensions aside, instead eager to fight, inside and outside, to achieve the important goals we set for the business. Most people (the vast majority, in my experience) will not do this. Instead, they may be fearful, need to be accepted socially, and may not be as equipped for the animosity and angst that a transformational change program will trigger.

I Know the Answers Exist

Undaunted leaders are visionary and inspirational—because they have to be. I am undaunted because I know that the answers I need exist within my reach. I may not know where exactly, but with thoughtfulness, research, engagement, and persistence…my team and I will find a way. Michelangelo described his sculpting technique as more of an unearthing process than some form of intuition: "Every block of stone has a statue inside it, and it is the task of the sculptor to discover it."

Almost every time that I have made a purely intuitive technology initial selection, without a discovery process, I have found myself changing direction. Putting my ego aside, I'm fine with making a pivot based on better information. Instead of dwelling on the challenges of the unknowns that must become known, I've honed a very detailed industry "Point of View" (POV) development process, which we will articulate in depth in Chapter 4. I still rely on my best judgment as to when I think I found the best solution to serve my need, but the innovation process starts with a judgment on where to begin the journey rather than intuiting the destination. I seek all the inputs I can, don't claim that my viewpoint is ever set in stone, and I iterate, communicate, and evolve my POV and that of the teams I lead through engagement with as many perspectives that I can find.

United States Marine Corps General James Mattis once penned, "Data not displayed is data not acted on."[12] If you were ever to see the walls surrounding the teams I lead, you will find a lot of pictures, some graphs, and hopefully some inspiration to share the data with your teams.

The best strategy at any time, and especially in times of immense change, is one that favors continuous learning, adjustment, and experimentation. You really must seek the data sets that describe your challenge and progress toward your goals. Those data are not a stagnant asset though: to make them useful you have to challenge what they are telling you. This process, supporting my intellectual curiosity and my focus on the positive outcomes for my constituents, helps to remove fears, uncertainties, and doubts, and frankly, mitigate ego. I surprise my friends and colleagues at times when I'm not afraid to ask them for a definition to a term or explain a concept that most would think I should know. I'll ask every time, rather than pretend to know and miss out on the full context of the discussion. Not knowing it all doesn't undermine my intelligence or ability to garner respect. It's more important for me to learn. I'm a weed—I'll take any source of education, information, and support to grow in any way that I can. As my mother says: "If it's man made, it can be

---

12   The Army Leader, *James Mattis's Leadership Philosophy*, www.
thearmyleader.co.uk/james-mattiss-leadership-philosophy/

man learned." This has surely been true in my experience. I have learned so much over the years that seemed so important at the time, only to have that knowledge usurped by yet another cycle of technology and innovation, all but obsoleting the previous.

"If people knew how hard I worked to get my mastery, it wouldn't seem so wonderful at all."

—Michelangelo

(Last Michelangelo quote. We promise.)

Fostering an Undaunted Team

Undaunted leaders will challenge themselves personally as well—to dig deep. At some point, you need to have the conviction to set and stick to your plan. We don't mean to doggedly execute a set plan in the face of changing new information—no, adjust your plan as you learn more. The goals are the goals. Those probably don't change as rapidly as the manner in which we proceed to attain them. The Undaunted Leader is confident in their ability to gain, assimilate, and utilize the bounty of information that exists around them and their teams. They lead from humility and a strong sense of purpose, because in doing so they create the room for this information to fully come to light and be useful: to create a common understanding of the challenges and opportunities in the markets and customer segments they aim to address. This is the root of forming a thoughtful point of view. Leading based on a principled approach further signals to the team that the leader is consistent, rational, open, and looking to lead within the team and not to simply drive them to some destination.

The destination is just as open for choice as much as the data supports it. In this way, the team truly is driving to a destination or some set of outcomes the team may participate in selecting themselves. By way of example, say you need to find a way to speed up the process for taking orders from your customers. This is a very common case faced by thousands of companies. You have many choices as to how to approach this challenge: should you rebuild your system, buy a new one, or use robotic process automation (RPA) to do the work of the people, while changing as little as possible in the company's business applications? This type of choice requires your entire team's thoughtful consideration, and by taking what they have to offer into consideration, they will be much more likely to fully embrace the critical challenges ahead. In many businesses, the destination is decided by the leadership and the team is simply tasked to row the boat toward that destination. If this approach is taken, **your team will not fully understand your expectation, because they have not participated in your journey; they can't fully share your mindset.**

In Chapter 3, we will explore the full set of leadership principles that the Undaunted Leader can draw upon to create organizational agility, enlist the very best intentions and support of their team, and embrace change. Adherence to principles offers a compelling way to overcome the undermining nature of skepticism and propagates an air of dauntlessness.

I have thought a lot about skepticism, as I have faced it constantly throughout my career. It's normal during times of great change to be skeptical. The problem is that many times this skepticism is formed on the basis of dated and unrelated experiences, a lack of understanding, a need to maintain the status quo, and ultimately fear. As for myself, when I feel skeptical, I seek an audience with people who can test me, who can play devil's advocate in a safe, offline environment (what happens in Vegas stays in Vegas) and test my points of view to their fullest extent. (In Chapter 5, we will codify this vetting process into something called a Red/Green debate.) I'll go where the data takes me; I'll challenge and test sources and thesis statements until I'm exhaustedly confident in their validity.

A 360° Review of the Undaunted Leader

I have done numerous 360-reviews in my life. This is a performance management approach that collects feedback on a leader from every angle of interaction: inside, outside, upwards, and downwards. I really don't like them too much as a tool to assess people performance within an organization in that they seem to encourage safety over progress. But, for the sake of clarity, let's conduct a 360-review on the model Undaunted Leader.

o Manager: You are highly regarded as a strategic asset, an abstract thinker that can be challenging to manage, but highly effective. You need to be coached at times about getting along with your peers, while at the same time will continue to be strongly encouraged to keep driving change.

o Peers: They like you if your objectives are aligned; their methods may make you uncomfortable at times, but you accept that rising tides raise all boats. If your objectives are *not* aligned, well, they are just a virus in the organization that must be isolated or purged.

o Reports: You create high-performance teams where everyone feels valued, respected, and supported. For those who don't want to come along, the Undaunted Leader must let them go for the sake of the overall team's performance.

o Self: I want to run fast—with scissors—too fast for the culture, it seems.

o Others: You are considered an outside-in thinker, recognized for keeping the big picture priorities in mind at all times, and known for getting stuff done.

I am not professing that to be an Undaunted Leader you have to measure up to this assessment. No, you don't. But having received aspects of this assessment myself at times in the context of different businesses and even international cultures, I can tell you that none of us work in a vacuum and that a good dose of self-awareness is critical as a leader. Just take this as an added insight as to how you may be perceived when taking an undaunted approach to leadership.

In Professor Lewin's studies of the "phenomena of group life," the text is littered with discussions of aggressive behaviors and patterns of rebellion against authority. Early experiments in social climates produced "more hypotheses than answers." It's somewhat fitting that as society and technology advances, we are still faced with the same conundrum.

ARE WE THERE YET?

"If you are working on something exciting that you really care about, you don't have to be pushed. The vision pulls you."

—*Steve Jobs*

If you have children, you've probably driven your kids on road trips when they were younger, to the calls of "are we there yet?". Given their age, you didn't feel like explaining geography or distance or traffic, and your punishment for your lack of servant leadership was incessant whining and mischief. Well, you can probably guess what I'm going to say next: why should your digital transformation be any different? Astonishingly, industry research houses will report in the same survey that most enterprises are committed to digital transformation, are progressing on-plan with their digital transformation, and have absolutely no idea how to define digital transformation (or have a dozen or more definitions, depending on who you are asking). Most lack a clear vision but instinctively know that change is required and so they embark on the journey without a map or compass. No wonder the outcomes of these journeys have varied widely. Always create a roadmap and plan that is vetted by the most trustworthy leaders of your business and then go about to accomplish it in a transparent manner.

And as the saying goes, if it were easy, I'd have done it already. Where does vision come from? For Steve Jobs and a handful of others, it may just come naturally. They just see it. I imagine that some people believe that having a vision in technology is akin to going into a meditative trance, having a lucid dream, or trying your luck with casting rune stones. Although I am not discounting any of those methods, for me, a vision emanates from a combination of intellectual curiosity and unbridled empathy.

We will dig deep into vision creation in Chapter 4, but after you have finished your controlled-breathing exercises, you need to turn your attention to becoming more (or even more) intellectually curious. If you are not today, then start right now! Look around you, observe, question the how's and the why's and challenge yourself to see it all in another way. Couple that with a very healthy dose of empathy.

I subscribe to the fundamental truth that you can only solve a problem if you can truly understand it. To understand, you must be curious, and you must have empathy. You need extreme empathy for those who are experiencing the problems you aim to solve. Empathy is all about putting yourself in the context and lives of others. With these two tools in hand, you now can understand the challenge and may be able to begin to postulate some potential solutions.

There is no substitute for technical knowledge and skills. Keep your tools sharp in this area! Read, experiment, build, go to meet-ups, tech talks, trade shows...whatever you need to do to stay current. Above all, listen and be interested in the experiences of those you aim to serve. This knowledge allows you to see the art of what's possible against the backdrop of the requirements (empathy) and potential solutions. Many times, your best teachers are those you are charged to lead.

It is extremely important to note that a vision is not an absolute truth, never to be modified. Your vision is the culmination of your thoughts on the topic area of interest. It is your current view on the path of evolution, one that you want to drive and create. As you learn more, your points of view will become more focused and your vision more complete and hopefully more compelling.

A FLASHLIGHT VERSUS A NORTH STAR

As we discussed, you have millennials that bring creativity but won't blindly follow the rules or the rulers. You have industry veterans that are fearless when it comes to scale and complexity but don't easily take a leap of faith on the untested. They both loathe mediocrity and yearn for the next intractable challenge. You are willing to take the time, do your homework, and create a plan. But if you build it, will they come (remember *Field of Dreams*)? Will they follow your vision, toward some set of shared goals and desired outcomes? Do you need to create a celestial industry vision that shines a light for all to see, or do you just need to provide the visionary flashlight for you and your team to use to cut through the commercial darkness and uncertainty you will doubtless face on your journey together?

Maybe you should be asking if they will follow YOU, as you march toward realizing your shared and co-created vision. Maybe not about building consensus on your points of view, but about the way you share the "how you got there." Transparency, authenticity, honesty, gratitude and trust. Maybe you need to think about all the ***principles of agile leadership*** required to lead a digital transformation program. Maybe there are leadership principles that both digital natives and digital pioneers can relate to.

3

PRINCIPLES FOR
TRANSFORMATIVE LEADERSHIP

This chapter was the most difficult for us to write. It is also perhaps the most meaningful and fundamental as well. We fully understand that it is hard to stick your neck out professionally, based on the experiences of others (like authors) that you don't know personally. We have taken great effort to scribe the backstories behind our observations, not because we think you will find them amusing (though we hope that you will), but to convey that we are not presenting theory or narrative.

After all the books we have read on leadership principles, writing this chapter in such a way as to make you stop and think requires us to create some new rules for business dogmatics—starting with the rule that we will vow to avoid pontification, platitudes, hyperbole, and banality. **Mediocrity is all too often tolerated in the business world—and that needs to end here.** We want to inspire change, in a simple and easy-to-apply manner, while staying true to the leadership traits that made you want to be a leader in the first place.

Our beliefs on leadership are founded on the following principles:

o Authenticity and Mission

o Trust

o Honesty

o Creativity

o Consistent and Positive

o Gratitude

o Vision and Purpose

How often do you ask whether others believe in you? How often do you ask whether you believe in yourself? Although these questions may seem rhetorical, simply asking them conveys a true interest in gaining understanding and self-awareness. If I were sitting next to you and asked you these simple questions as we discussed the principles of agile leadership, would you not feel more engaged? I would only ask you if I were curious and truly interested, and chances are if I didn't, I would never have the opportunity to learn from you. Engage in not only a self-discovery on these principles, but in a vested conversation with those you lead, and the floodgates will open to a more connected and ful-filling relationship for you all.

That question of believability influences more than just your team and colleagues. In a digital economy, the sphere of leadership extends beyond the four walls of an organization, to ecosystems of partners who will demand transparency before letting you play in their platform sandbox, and to consumers who you may have little to no direct interaction with as your offers are embedded and sold by other vendors. The days of the linear producer-consumer relationships ("you eat what I serve") are going the way of the buggy whip. Now, too, the judgments you make, on what you make, have ramifications and consequences on society at large. Successes will go viral without your stimulus, and mistakes can compound exponentially, beyond your reach and conception.

In a platform or shared economy, you may not know exactly how your products and services are used across a variety of markets. This means that your vision must somehow be codified, most likely now literally into code—into software or technology—and that code will be written by teams that will follow your vision and your leadership based on the principles you exhibit and reward.

In her book *The Art of Relevance*, Smithsonian author and visionary, Nina Simon relates the challenge of staying relevant in the digital economy to transparency and authenticity:

> *Relevance is not something an institution can assign by fiat. Your work matters when it matters to people—when THEY deem it relevant, not you. [E]mpathize with their concerns and interests, and develop authentic ways to invite them into your work on their own terms.*[13]

So, let's take a look at each of the leadership principles that we have found to be vital to improving the agility and cultural shift necessary to drive digital transformation. Rather than opine about blueprints and prescriptions for agile leadership, we would rather present our observations and anecdotes and leave it to you to determine how these principles relate to you and your work. We do so recognizing that you are unique in the world, and likewise, your business challenges will be unique. Which principles you need to apply and how to apply them will draw on your leadership capabilities and experiences. There's no magic formula here or killer app for leadership…there's only you. Our goal is to help you build your leadership recipe, with a greater appreciation for the attributes you will add to your own unique leadership mosaic.

---

[13]   Nina Simon, *The Art of Relevance*, (Museum 2.0, 2016)

AUTHENTICITY AND MISSION

People can immediately see the difference between someone who is authentic and someone who is not. This is just an innate human instinct in my opinion. (Having said that, I think my dog has a pretty good sense of authenticity as well.) I've had many personal and professional encounters where I just knew that the person sitting in front of me was not the one I was being shown. Many times, people put on a persona that they believe will be to their benefit in establishing how they want to be seen or perceived. There are many problems with doing this, but chief among them is that people just don't buy it. The slightest insincerity or inconsistency can very quickly undermine someone's belief in a leader, or the desire to engage with them.

Your authenticity as a leader of digital natives and giants will be particularly scrutinized as the digital world is filled with deceit. With so much information throughout our digital lives, it can be very difficult to find the simple truth. Computer scientists are trained that digital objects aren't just bits that travel in space and time, but content that must be authenticated by the software that renders them. Digital natives grew up in a world where you can swipe right to signify instant approval or rejection. Your company brand is facing the same challenge in the digital era: consumers crave transparency, respect, and consistency. The antiquated practice of extracting money from consumers through fear and persuasion is dying on the vine of personalization and social engagement.

"My mission in life is to make people happy."

—Walt Disney

Authenticity is about leading from your core values and beliefs. For me, I also need to have a mission that I'm committed to. We all have many interests and personal missions that hold our attention and focus. A mission in business is really no different, as I see it. For example, I have been on a mission for over twenty-five years to help modernize the telecommunications service providers, in terms of their operational effectiveness and competitiveness. This mission comes from my fundamental belief that these companies have created a true social good for the world and that we (the world) need them or their successors to be successful in order that human society may continue to march toward a brighter and more sustainable, empathetic, and kinder future for us all.

I have now generalized my mission to enable organizations to strike the right balance between automation and personalization. Too much automation and we are left with a hollow and maybe valuable but impersonal and non-sticky customer experience. Not enough automation, and we may not be permitted to operate long-term, due to the effect of unfavorable economics and slowness in serving an ever-more demanding customer. I am on a mission to help find and optimize this balance for the companies and customers I serve. Artificial intelligence (AI) need not be a scary and fully disruptive technology if applied with common sense, respect, and a laser focus on value creation over cost cutting alone.

The Genesis of My Mission

The year was 1987, and I was young and very motivated to improve my lifestyle, as I was in the second year of my college experience at DeVry University in Columbus, Ohio. I had enrolled in their Electrical Engineering Technology program. At DeVry at this time, students joined a program that met either in the mornings or evenings and with all the classes predetermined for three years. One of the required classes I took was named something like "Communications Systems." The professor was a much older, genteel man, and he not only was proficient in the communications technologies of those days, but moreover, he had a passion for them and the value they brought then and over the decades. This professor had worked for many years for

AT&T Bell Labs. He would share relevant stories about how the technologies introduced by the Labs had changed the world and delivered even greater social benefits. WOW, this really spoke to me. Maybe I could be part of that mission. Maybe I could someday make my contributions to the ever-expanding field of communications technology and maybe, just maybe, I could make the world a little more connected and civil.

From that point on, although I took many other classes and reconsidered my mission several times, the communications business really stuck with me as my most preferred field of employment.

Fast forward a few years, and I had three job offers in front of me as I looked toward graduation. And two of them were with Bell Labs! I remember the interviews and trips to the two locations vividly. I had all but decided to go to Bell Labs as my preferred choice of employment. The recruiter told me, "You have the option to join the International R2 MFC 5ESS signaling group, or the Audix ISDN group." What did all that mean? Everyone around me seemed to just know exactly what this all meant, and so at least that was comforting. I chose to join the position in the International 5ESS group because it had the opportunity to really improve the world's connectivity for voice communications. It directly aligned with my mission.

The first day came and I had moved from Ohio to Naperville, Illinois, rented an apartment, bought a few new outfits, and gotten a tight haircut. Prior to this, my hair was very long, and I was rocking that 1980's mullet. Bell Labs basically put you back into school for a while, soon after you were onboarded. There were many things a developer really needed to understand, to be able to be effective in this job setting. This period was thrilling and my mentor was a trusting colleague and very solid technologist. After a short while, the assignment became maintenance programming and then feature development, and then onto taking on the ownership for entire projects or subsystems. Again, I met amazing friends, mentors, officemates, and colleagues.

I quickly realized that I could, in fact, do this job and I could develop software on this amazing system called the 5ESS. That said, I believed that you needed to be committed to your craft, and so I needed to become a great C programmer. More importantly than that, I was working among some of the most talented computer scientists in the world, whereas my degree was in electronics engineering technology. So, within six months of starting my new job, I signed up for night school at North Central College with the goal to receive a Master of Science in Computer Science. Bell Labs would support employees' educational goals via tuition reimbursement. Wow, all I had to do was do the work and get the grades (while I was still adjusting to this new work environment). Two years later, I had a Masters in Computer Science and was one of the trusted members of our team.

A mission can really drive you forward, and authenticity and commitment build the type of relationships you need to be successful as a person, let alone a technologist or leader. So, what motivates you? Money is not a mission—it is a desirable result, but hopefully not the purpose. I have met some of the most miserable, highly wealthy people, with no clear mission in life—no joy. Finding your mission requires some contemplation, maybe some tools, maybe some advice. Seek out a career or life coach (it's easy to be skeptical, but their job is to help you look in the mirror and take you out of your comfort zones). Perhaps you can try writing a personal manifesto, of what you know to be true, what you believe to be true, and what you want to be true in life.

Face the difficult choices and obstacles you will encounter to bring your work in alignment with your mission, and joy will follow, as will success.

I recall a great conversation I had with my friend, colleague, and boss at one time, who was the CEO of Telcordia Technologies. We were talking about how a particular technology that I was passionate about could be applied to solve our customers' challenges. I would pitch the benefits and characteristics of this solution, and how it would help us do something important and bring value; he would come back at me with a sober New York cynicism, and we would just spin. After about an hour he said, "Oh! You're the worst kind of CTO—you're a true believer!" *Yes, I Am.* That was my mission coming through, with my passion and willingness to listen, learn, and innovate.

TRUST

People will believe in you if you believe in yourself and your mission. I have embarked on many journeys that I truly believed would have a positive outcome for myself and my team, yet, in business or in life—*it is possible to do everything right and still fail!* People somewhat know that. How do you overcome that natural and logical skepticism, such that your team will follow you into the battles ahead? Perhaps you get them seventy-five percent of the way there with a strong vision, a specificity of desired outcomes, and technology enablers. Perhaps the last twenty-five percent, for them to take that leap of faith, is just plain trust. "Look, gang, we are facing tough odds here, and we may fail, but I am committed to making this a success and I will not deceive you on the challenge ahead."

It is possible to do everything right and still fail!

Trust is earned in the trenches. It can't be mandated or delegated, and unfortunately, once broken is almost impossible to repair. How will your teams assess your trustworthiness? Trust is knowing that your leader or peer will absolutely only act in the best interest of the business and in you as an employee (even when those interests might conflict, such as in a workforce reduction due to poor financial results). *"I don't really believe, but I want you to"* is a leadership sin that I place on the top of my list of what not to do!

How do leaders demonstrate trustworthiness then, in an unfavorable business environment? I think this starts with being clear in expectations, open to feedback, consistent in behavior, and honest. There is also a tribal aspect to trust in a business setting. Have you ever heard the phrase "I can talk bad about my brother, but you had better not dare"? The implication being that family, and business organizations, have one another's back. If they don't, then who will?

Let's take, for example, a person with whom I had once worked, who had many of the makings of a good leader, was focused on the business, was very likable, and talked of valuing trustworthiness. At one point, we began to work more closely, as I was called in to help introduce a new business and establish a new culture in our organization. I was given the assignment to conduct a significant piece of primary research that would serve as the strategic backing for our new business. As I went about my assignment, I had many occasions to share the work in progress with the company's broader leadership team. Well, wouldn't you know it, not everyone appreciated the strategy, and not everyone felt comfortable with the degree of change implied in taking the company in the direction we were recommending. So, I started getting feedback from my boss that his peers thought I believed that I was the "smartest guy in the room," and that several of them just plain did not like me.

I wasn't sure what to make of these seemingly unconstructive criticisms. I had never received feedback in a business setting that "people did not like me." I admit that I can be a bit of an egg-head at times and that I can be intensely interested in technical topics that maybe others would find tedious. That's just part of what makes me...me. I really enjoy the technology or topics I find interesting, and I will fuss on them to the degree of knowing all that I can before moving on. My boss knew that; it's why he sought my expertise.

Yet, when his peers gave him challenging feedback that they did not understand or agree with some of the content of the research, he just appeared to accept it from them without defending the work. Worse yet, he did not afford me an opportunity to even hear their concerns directly. So, I set a meeting with the senior leaders of the business to hear it for myself: long story short, it turned out that much of the critique had actually been leveled at my boss and he had used me and the project as a scapegoat. Trust broken!

So, I had breakfast with them a few weeks later and told them that I expected their support, instead of passive acceptance of personal insults toward me or politicized feedback on my work. They took that pretty well and said, "We need to do a better job of demonstrating support of you and your work." I thought that was a pretty good response. Heck, I had lost trust in them, I called them on it, and they responded in a humble and considerate manner. I half-expected my critique to be met with denial, rejection, and negativity. But I was pleasantly surprised that they just took the critique and moved on. So, although my trust in them had been shaken, I continued to press on in our objective and kept the pressure on my work and our change plan for the business.

Trust is the basis for any relationship of merit. Many of us first learned about the importance of trust while participating in a team sport or group activity. For me, it was playing football in high school, where a quarterback would either take charge and lead his teammates into battle, or would blame others for his failures, which undermined their desire to put their bodies on the line and could even result in the occasional look-out block (as in, oops, I may have intentionally tripped on this blade of grass, so "Look Out!" for that linebacker charging your way).

A leader needs the support and willingness of their team in order to succeed, and demanding it or whining about performance is not a recipe for success.

Trust starts with the foundation of intellectual honesty. If a person starts off by misrepresenting the facts of a matter, then trust in that individual is impossible. In today's world of connected devices and experiences, the facts are available to all. In business, the facts will require the legwork and analysis to derive them. There is likely no news feed that reports on the latest moves of your competitors or the advancements within your customers or markets. Gaining this information requires research, consideration, and engagement. Once we have the information, then we need to be willing to openly debate and consider it. We must be able and willing to trust that we can do so openly. As time moves forward and our understanding deepens, we must also be willing to adjust our perspectives. Just taking these steps within a team can serve as a powerful platform for a shared understanding and the establishment of trust.

Have you ever worked with individuals who hold on tight to information? I have, and I can certainly tell you that their choice to do so did not instill a sense of trust and collaboration with me. I operate as an "open book" in the teams that I lead and the companies that my teams have supported. This means simple things like publishing your plan. Publish your roadmap; make available your research. The old adage "information is power" has not served us well in the era of digital transformation. No, I'd offer, "shared information creates shared understanding and trust."

When I join a new company, I first go into a period of trying to understand all that I can. Imagine my executive office covered in giant sticky notes and meetings with all my peers and reports as I work to first understand. From this, my next step is to translate this understanding into a sharable form as I review it again with my teams and stakeholders...this alone has proven a key method of forming trust. I am open to feedback and changing my perspectives along the way until I get to a view that most people see as also true and accurate.

The steps that follow are described in detail in Chapter 4, but once a point of view is established and plan created by the team, it becomes the team's plan and point of view and we literally hang it on the walls, post it to our intranet, and hold sharing sessions for all who want to join in and challenge and improve it.

From the employee's perspective, trust is just as critical, and the loss of it is very difficult to communicate safely, let alone recover from. *I have your back* is critical in companies and competitive business environments, and without it, progress will be very slow, and the impact of any contributor will be muted. Fear of reprisal is a potent poison to progress and innovation.

Fear of reprisal is a potent poison
to progress and innovation.

We all need to make difficult decisions that come with consequences and trade-offs every day. Should we invest in the new technology or should we partner for it? Should I take that fourth week of travel in a row to represent my company at a conference in a controversial session, even though it's not really my responsibility? In all of these decisions, some people will be supportive, while others will not for whatever reason. In order to be able to make these decisions, we need to trust that our leadership will support us regardless of the outcome, as long as we perform within the agreements we have made. I need to know that when a conflict arises with a customer or competitor, leadership will recognize the challenge and have my back against the naysayers.

HONESTY

It has been said that "everything I need to know to be a good leader, I learned in kindergarten."[14] Okay, this may be too far an oversimplification, but author Robert Fulghum was onto something, by focusing our attention on the Golden Rule ("Do unto others as you would have them do unto you"), and the simple basic principles of decency and mutual respect. How can you lead an organization to greatness if you don't respect the employees enough to be honest with them?

---

[14] Robert Fulghum, *All I Really Need to Know I Learned in Kindergarten: Uncommon Thoughts on Common Things* (New York, Villard Books, 1988)

It's far too easy, given our hierarchical, climb-the-ladder organizational structures, and proclivity for restructuring, reorganization, and redundancies, for many leaders to quickly get caught up in their business responsibilities and forget that they need to be good and honest people first. Without this basic characteristic, employees will quickly catch on that something is not right—that there is an inconsistency between what is being asked and that which is being displayed.

Our employees have us under a constant microscope. Most of them have been burned at least once in their careers. I have heard and witnessed people who, on the heels of a positive performance review, are terminated. The separation usually comes as a surprise (typically a Friday morning impromptu call with a manager, HR, and a third person who never introduces themselves—aka, Legal).

Even as leaders, we're no different. I find myself, at times, wondering what the people I have worked for are really up to. When the words coming out of their mouths just don't ring true, or when the optimism doesn't line up with the financial results, that's when I usually begin to consider making a move to greener pastures: not over the financial trouble, but because someone either doesn't think I can handle the brutal truths or just finds it easier to smile in the hallways and let HR do the dirty work down the road.

In some organizations, people have learned that honesty only begets more scrutiny. I once worked in a leadership team where the CEO was brutally honest, but his direct reports had learned over the years to be guarded in what they share, and when needed, to simply not share at all. The weekly leadership meeting always started the same way: the agenda was posted, general items were discussed, and then the deep dive topics were round-tabled. As each business leader began to share their update you could just feel the sandbagging from sales and the "happy talk" from the product managers (grinning at us and passively agreeing while they are actively planning to do otherwise), and the ultimate kick-the-can-down-the-road closing of the meeting.

This, of course, was not the desired outcome for this expense of precious time.[15]

This leadership team had learned to become guarded, and, in some sense, to hide their problems. In previous years, they had received little in the way of honest, supportive management, let alone any empathy when asking for help. Instead, they had been only weighed and measured. And they had learned that providing too much data made the measurement more severe.

By the time the new CEO arrived, and I came on the scene, the culture was well conditioned to this dynamic. We tried to turn the culture on a dime. We tried to preach for the need for open and honest communications and metrics, we shared our plan and strategy openly, and took all feedback seriously, adjusting as we gained more experience. And most importantly, we aimed to simply be honest and transparent in our dealings with the top leaders of the company.

But what perhaps had greater influence was the expectations of our employees on the new CEO and his leadership team. Internal communications remained stoic, month after month, while employees were bombarded with rumor mills and skepticism from industry analysts and customers over our survival as an independent software vendor. I can recall many "all-hands meetings" where the same questions were asked month after month to different leaders, regarding our future. The employees would quickly take notice of any difference in substance—software engineers are trained to look for any anomalies—and then the

---

[15] A side note on the role of IT systems: The brutal truths behind your business are only as good as the data on your operations that can be shared and analyzed. In this leadership meeting, we aimed to have a real fact-based discussion on how we should best run this business. Without real data in everyone's hands, only arm's length or abstract recommendations were possible. The financially significant challenges were hardly ever on the table as that would have required a degree of insight and transparency that was simply difficult to catalyze given the walled gardens of data across the organization.

damage control would be put in place to clean up any misunderstandings or major disparities in the message. The leadership team figured out that it was probably easier to just speak the truth than to try to remember and reconcile all the *versions* of the truth across the organization. This became the new normal for the most part.

The hardest threshold in honesty with staff is faced when it comes to financial results and other non-disclosed proprietary data. We ask our teams to work diligently, to pull our organizations out of a financial quagmire, but then we won't tell them what's wrong such that they can go out and fix it. I have always believed that the best choice is to just stick to the truth and be as transparent as you can. I know that leaders may feel they are taking a risk by sharing sensitive information with their team. I aim to change the culture of the company by example; and what example do I set by declaring that "things are going to be different now," and then removing all the numbers from my staff meeting PowerPoint slides?

We talked about trust already. You're starting to see how these principles go hand in hand. I trust my teams—I truly respect them—enough that I could be fully transparent with them.[16] My group became very tightly knit around a shared view of the business. We knew exactly where the gaps were, what our goals should be, when we were succeeding, and where we were failing. I never had to invoke any "Management-By-Nike" project

---

[16] I am not advocating that as a leader you can or should share everything that is going on inside or outside the business. Many times, you simply cannot do so, due to legal restrictions, and in those cases make sure to explain why exactly; we take for granted that someone writing code for a living understands all the regulatory restrictions and protections that govern our disclosures. That said though, we need to treat our employees like adults who have the absolute right to be informed, so they may make the best decisions they can for themselves.

edicts—*Just Do It*—as my crew already knew why we needed something to be implemented before I even asked.

I have had several of the same people on my teams join me at new employers. This, I believe, is in part due to my commitment to, and expectation of, honesty. This includes companies that were in the midst of organizational upheaval, where loyalty and integrity were tested to the max. But how does this principle apply when you are not just facing chaos, but you've run head-on into a brick wall?

The company where I first held the role of CTO was sold in an asset sale weeks after we officially shut down. Timing was just not on our side, as the telecom meltdown of 2000 was just too much for the little software company to bear. I still vividly remember going to the office on our last day of operations, where I met with each of my employees, told them what was happening, and then formally severed their employment. After some serious discussions with HR and Legal, we agreed that we would be honest and to the point throughout the notification process. So, the last day started alongside my great colleague and friend, intoning: "Unfortunately, due to the downturn in the telecoms market, we are shutting down operations and your employment is ending today." After doing this about sixty times that day, I signed my own severance agreement and walked out the door.

These encounters could have been brutal (for all parties involved), had not each of our employees been truthfully informed of the situation during the entire year leading up to the closure. They knew we were in the fight for the life of the company and we were all committed as a team to the bitter end.

The (not so) funny part, was that the week before the shutdown a consultant showed up at my office to hear all about our great technology. At least this was the premise, but we all knew they were there to try to maintain the value of the software assets upon the close of the business. Sensing the irritation from my colleagues, I asked them to just level with us and to be honest and open about their objectives. I told him that we would be happy to show him the keys to the software, the documentation, the tools, etcetera…after all, it was and always had been the property of the company. This made the consultant very uncomfortable, and they never did own up to the true objective of the meetings. We handed them everything anyway and I coached my team to be honest, open, and transparent: we were principled all the way.

The drop-the-mic moment came two weeks after shutdown, when I received a call from the new leader of the business. He was the only employee and had the remit to sell the assets, and had realized that without the development team, the software was of very little value. He was calling to see if I would rejoin him with this task and help him to proffer the assets. Needless to say, I respectfully declined. Had they simply been honest, I am sure we could have managed to help them to achieve their asset sale targets.

o Ben Franklin was renowned for saying that "Honesty is the best policy."

o The Girl Scout Law starts with, "I will do my best to be honest and fair…"

o Fairy tales instill, "Long ago there was a boy who was honest and sincere…"

o And in business, we are held to a higher standard: The Sarbanes-Oxley Act of 2002!

CREATIVITY

It's Monday morning, and I'm sitting in a conference room in New Jersey. I flew in the night before from Chicago and had no plans, except to find a meal and get to my hotel for some rest so that I could be at my best the next morning. My mind was racing as I thought about the decision I had made and what the next day would be like. I had just joined Telcordia Technologies as the

CTO of the next generation Operations Support Systems (OSS) group. Telcordia, which was formerly known as Bellcore, was essentially the gold-standard company in OSS before the breakup of AT&T into the Bell System operating companies. Bellcore was a research consortium (shortened from Bell Communications Research) that was owned collectively by the Baby Bells. Bellcore was a shared resource, responsible for providing all the operating systems, standards, training, and the like for all the local operating companies.

As a developer at Bell Labs, I had taken training from Bellcore and just saw them as the heart of the telecommunications industry; they made sure that everything in the networks and services provided would just work. After the Baby Bells were allowed to compete under regulatory reforms, Bellcore was forced to shed its Bell name and had to transform overnight into a free-standing commercial organization, renamed Telcordia Technologies. Telcordia then became the buffer between the former Bell operating networks and the horde of equipment vendors with a multitude of proprietary systems. Earlier in my career, as the Head of Software Development for OSS at Tellabs Network Solutions Group, I saw Telcordia as the organization that ensured that all the equipment that Tellabs made, and the management systems my teams were developing, would interoperate with other vendor equipment in our customers' networks. By the time that I joined Telcordia myself, I, needless to say, came in with real respect and appreciation for the organization.

Just prior to joining Telcordia, I had been working for the up-and-comer competition, Cramer Systems. Cramer was sold to Amdocs and I left a few years after that transaction, but my colleagues and I at Cramer and Amdocs had really given Telcordia a run for their money, and we had really disrupted their business along the way. It did not help that Telcordia had been sold a few times and was owned by a mix of private equity and venture capital holders. That, along with the competition that my company had brought, the changing dynamic of their customers, and the financial pressure from their owners, had pushed Telcordia into a decline of revenue that had persisted for several years. At the time I joined the organization, I came in with the technical respect and admiration of old, but my rose-colored glasses were a bit foggy after witnessing firsthand their struggles with commercialization.

I was hired by an executive who had been given the challenge to introduce a so-called "next generation" portfolio of applications, so that the company could return to growth while leveraging the incumbency they had long held. The new group was essentially a collection of software platforms aimed at modernizing the portfolio of the existing business, to match the capabilities of emerging communications technologies and services. Many of the next generation platforms were acquired from other smaller companies, and the integration into the mothership had been difficult. The cultures were not congruent, the larger business was funding everything, and the board wanted measurable results immediately. I joined right into the pressure cooker that was the promise of this next-generation business unit.

Even with this cloud hanging over the organization, one amazing thing about Telcordia was the depth of knowledge and value they had consistently placed on education and skill. The teams were tight-knit and focused on delivery and support of their customers. The systems they had built were, and still are, supporting the operation of a vast amount of the US telecommunications network, so the stakes were always high, and so were the expectations.

Their legacy business, including a network inventory record-keeping system that was using some of the original code from 1969, was proud, and rightfully so. They were the giants whose shoulders the rest of us were standing on—and I knew it. All this said, the new business needed to grow, and the customers needed fresher technology. Telcordia had tried many strategies to replace their own legacy, and leverage their own incumbency, but these attempts had all fallen short in one way or another.

I came into the game with an "At Cramer, we did it this way," and "I think we need to try a different approach," and "what if we tried a radical solution," as ways to explore the edges of what was possible at Telcordia. Many, many times my questions would be met with essentially the same response: "We tried that before, and it failed, and therefore we don't want to do it again." Being the CTO and focused on innovation, this response was disheartening to say the least. I came here to get this portfolio sorted and to get the business growing.

So, this Monday morning after my badge was printed and I met my team, I was faced with the reality that the company was tired of the trial and error that had led to the current situation, and that there was no consensus that the change intended for my business unit was even worth doing.

I wanted to just press on anyway, but I would need a creative and novel approach, in order to develop a credible strategy that would return us to growth. We needed a process that was rooted in bringing in the external perspective of our customers. (We will take a deep dive on this approach in Chapter 4.) We started our journey by engaging with the market and working to form a series of perspectives that would ultimately become the roots of our strategy. Many of those customer, and prospective customer, meetings were difficult, as there was a lot of history, both good and bad, to unwind before we could get to talking about the future.

We created a unique vision for the industry that was based on the reality of our customers, and not that of ourselves. My assessment of Telcordia was, that like many legacy vendors (think BlackBerry, when operating as Research In Motion), we had become too inwardly focused and driven. That's a predictable hazard for enterprise-driven software development, where you have to develop product requirements years in advance of your customers even knowing what problems they will have that need solving.

We shared this externally focused vision within and outside our OSS business unit, and we made sure to continually test and tweak our points of view externally as well. This creative, "outside-in approach" was able to win over some internal skeptics—those who were able to see that we *didn't know what we didn't know*—and who wanted to join us on the vision work we were undertaking, by incorporating the program into their daily business lives.

One of the most powerful leadership techniques that we invented at this time, at least as shared by my team, was that we literally banned the phrase "we tried that and failed and thus don't want to try it again." If you said that in a meeting, I showed you the door. Eventually, the non-creative participants stopped coming to the portfolio planning sessions. My team reported that the elimination of this blocking factor (they used other words for it), streamlined the idea-to-implementation and product launch processes in a measurable way.

As for my personal takeaway, I stopped talking about previous experiences, and instead favored the market voice and the voice of our customers, to make the case for our innovations and changes in strategy.

My mother tells me that "people and organizations are like rubber bands...you can stretch them, but they have a tendency to snap back to the way they were before you started." My life experiences have yet to prove her wrong. It sounds cliché to say it, but **change is hard**. Change is really hard when you have a history of success in your business or a history of failure in a new business or strategy. Every signal you get from the organization and from your view of your collective history tells you just to keep executing on the previously successful strategy, in favor of entertaining a new one. Some popular business books will tell you to see your business strategy as a series of waves or horizons, where the horizons represent the changes you plan to make and the new business you will have as a result. But if the organization does not realize or truly believe that it *must change* in order to survive or thrive, getting anywhere past the steady-state is difficult and fraught with setbacks and retrenchments, in the comfort of the existing business model.

> *"Creativity is just connecting things. When you ask creative people how they did something, they feel a little guilty because they didn't really do it, they just saw something. It seemed obvious to them after a while. That's because they were able to connect experiences they've had and synthesize new things."[17]*

—Steve Jobs

Creativity is not the same as either imagination or gut feel. Creativity is informed, based on knowledge and experience. The customers' voice, thoroughly researched, analyzed, and pondered, may represent the most powerful voice to drive your business. Keep in mind that I am not advocating that you do everything your customers ask you to do, nor that you should take their point of view as your own without considering your own competencies and vision. I am advocating that you actively seek the customer's point of view and that you take it to heart outside of the context of their history with you or their specific organizational structures. In my experience, customer organizational structures, and the internal political environment that it creates, can distort their intentions into politically acceptable strategies that may be a big compromise from their true objectives. So, take caution to hear the customer, but listen with an ear for the value they are aiming to create, the competition they face, the constraints they have, and the organizational politics of the people you are speaking with. If this is not active listening, I don't know what is.

Take the feedback and assess whether it fits your researched point of view: if it does, challenge it and see if there are nuances that may have been missed; if the feedback is incongruent, you may have missed something or perhaps the specifics of this customer

---

17   Gary Wolf, "Steve Jobs: The Next Insanely Great Thing," *WIRED*, February 1, 1996, www.wired.com/1996/02/jobs-2/

have created the need for a specific approach for them. Either way, listen, learn, and iterate. Your goal is to create or unlock value for your customers, preferably before a competitor or a disruptor finds it. Keep in mind that the value of your creativity will be judged in the eye of the buyer. If you cannot trace the path between your amazing new technology and some reason that either a person or a corporation will get value from, then you really need to question the reasons why you are making the investments in creating your product or technology.

Creativity is taking center stage now, under the spotlight of digital transformation. Creativity can be the difference between merely replacing a call center agent with a bot-based customer service portal, versus exposing your key business processes to customers who can build and execute an offer in your systems that will address their individual needs. Many organizations will attempt digital transformation at their edges: they will begin to offer digital interactions with their customers or bundle services with ecosystem partners for sake of convenience. I believe that kind of vision is too narrow. Focusing on self, they will inevitably struggle to get out of their own way.

But those who can see their business as a platform to deliver value to their customers, based on the skills and competencies they can uniquely deliver, will relentlessly apply creativity to solve problems that their customers thought were intractable or problems that they didn't even know they had. Those are the companies that will truly transform.

And once in a while, rare as it may be, we stumble on a vision-driven product idea or transformative concept that will change the world. For the great inventors who created lightning in a bottle in the absence of a customer, my hat is off to you all. For the rest of us, we need to channel creativity through a customer-vetted vision, earning their trust (and remuneration) by providing them a measurable improvement to the business or lifestyle.

CONSISTENT AND POSITIVE

Early in my leadership apprenticing days, I worked for a very charismatic and highly intelligent leader. He was the kind of guy that you just wanted to be around and spend time with, regardless of the environment or setting. He always made me feel like he had a vision and that my contributions were essential to realizing it. In short, he was a great visionary leader with all the best communications skills—all packaged up in a thoughtful, educated, and worldly force of nature.

During our time together, he was the head of the organization and I was his senior director of product management. We had a vision, funding, interested customers, but were seen as a bit orthogonal to the core business of the overall company. From our perspective, what we were building was just as critical in driving the operations of the world's networks in an efficient and profitable manner. Our business unit was a startup business within a much larger and highly successful organization; from the larger organization's perspective though, our technology was there to throw into a sales pitch as a necessary, but optional, feature of the overall solution. This fracturing became more and more pronounced as our technology became more sophisticated and the sales became larger in magnitude, which drove the ongoing and increasing need for more features and capability.

I had worked as a senior technologist in the core business for years prior to joining this new team. I had helped to build the systems we sold, and as a result, I had a very solid reputation within the larger organization; they had accepted and valued my work and contributions, and I truly respected them and the work we had done together. I had assumed that my reputation for being a thoughtful engineer would be a solid asset as I moved into our startup side business. And I thought that our visionary leader knew this as well.

As our business progressed, the tensions between our business unit and the larger enterprise grew. I really did not understand why this was the case. After all, we were all working for the same company with the same goals! We sold to the same customers, our stock options were the same, and we certainly had the same hungry competitors.

The issues that caused the most pressure were the common ones: unrealistic expectations; limited investment while giving away (bundling) our technology; and the standard competition between business units for shared resources and attention. Or so that was the way the strife was rationalized.

The real and underlying issue was far more surprising. Our leader, the guy that we all loved, often treated his peers in the larger business with ZERO respect. None. Zero. For all the great attributes on full display for his team, the inverse was conveyed to his peers and their staff. Once he stepped foot into a conference room, the benevolent and encouraging leader that we experienced gave way to a seemingly unforgiving and unsympathetic combatant amongst his peer group. We would have a meeting amongst our team where he would encourage us on the company's path to success, and then take us to a cross-business meeting where he would excoriate the limitations of the core business team and diminish the value of their work.

While our leader must have believed he was fighting on our behalf, his inconsistent approach served only to undermine the trust we all needed to be successful.

We had to collaborate with the core business. We had to work with our colleagues on a daily basis to service our shared customers. Though I had left the core business with a solid reputation, I quickly found myself walking a tightrope between the two organizations and I was sure that some of my working relationships suffered.

Though we had tried to share our concerns with him, it was difficult to constructively convey the impact of this communications approach on organizational performance. Ultimately, he left the company and in turn left our team in a more difficult political environment. Rather than use his departure as an opportunity to mend fences, the leadership from the core business took over the team and I ended up resigning, as did several of my colleagues. **Faith lost is difficult to regain.**

Why is consistency on this list of undaunted leadership principles?

o Consistency demonstrates clearly your commitment to your principles

o Consistency gives people a reason to seek out your leadership

People need to know what to expect and how you will treat them when they knock on your office door or schedule that video meeting—no matter who they might be.

Have you ever met a technology person who looks a bit different than the rest of the crowd, who keeps to themselves, and generally seems only interested in what's in front of them or in fantasy games and coding? I know a lot of them, and I can tell you that although they may look and act a bit differently, these folks are just as deep and complex as anyone else. What motivates one person may be completely of no interest to another. I think this is in fact quite wonderful and makes life and work so much more interesting.

I'm not playing on a stereotype here, since the boom of the Internet and now cloud computing, it's cool to be a geek! We come in many forms now, including the hipster geek, the smart old dude, the tattooed everywhere system admin, and even the buttoned-up, clean-cut developer. Regardless of the many and varied types of people you may work with, all of them will respond to your positivity, your interest in them, and the consistency in which you present yourself.

I really believe that everyone goes to work in the morning with the intent to accomplish something meaningful and to do a good job. If we go into the office and our mood as a leader is sour, or we are inconsistent, chances are pretty high that we will spread this vibe across our teams, and in the end, leave them less productive and less motivated. If we are inconsistent, many people will simply avoid interaction for fear of our unpredictability (of which we may not even be aware). That, too, leads to a less productive environment and prevents the team from engaging fully, sharing, and contributing to the success of your work and projects.

I have experienced very clear examples of both the positive and consistent leader model, and unfortunately the converse.

I had the great opportunity to join a company focused on analytics and the Internet-of-Things delivered as a service. This company had really figured out a repeatable and highly valuable niche. Unfortunately, the software platforms, operations environment, and innovation required a much greater level of investment than had been available for the previous years.

I joined to help them scale their business, which meant that we would need to dramatically increase the capacity of the systems, while we introduced more analytical tools and professional services.

This is where I met Luke and John. John was a guy who was all about getting stuff done and he had a real "motor" to his persona—his word, not mine. Every morning, John would hold a *Hill Street Blues* style standup meeting (picture a police shift commander at a podium issuing the orders for the day) in our operations area. He had a massive board of stuff to get done, and a set of clear owners who would be responsible for working the action items, and who would be accountable for their completion. Each day, John came into the meeting positive and clear, and at the end of the session would say something like "Go and do good." Same thing each day, and the result of his positivity and clarity was that everyone in the room knew what to expect and that their work would be appreciated, challenged, and visible each day. These meetings were not all easy, we definitely had conflicts, and some tasks that were more frustrating than others. But regardless, John had mastered this cadence and had built a culture of performance and accountability.

I would join these meetings as much as I could, to listen in and to answer any questions that would come up. Mostly though, I joined to show the team that I was "all-in" with them, and that I supported them regardless. Within a month or so of joining,

John, Luke, and I had decided that we would move our entire business to the Cloud and that we would do it in a "Lift and Shift" approach. Our "Get to the Cloud" project was going to fill John's whiteboard day after day with transformative actions that were going to test his cadence.

Luke had been with the company for much of its life and he had faced the 1.0 challenge and every other challenge each day since. Luke had hired John and was accountable for all technology before I joined. Luke was definitely the true believer in the technology and the business model and was also a great manager. By the time I joined, there was some real worry that I would be the new guy to come in and change everything up and potentially even displace the current leaders. That was the farthest thing from my mission. Luke had weathered the storms and had built a solid team and was keeping them motivated each day by being a great manager and person, but also by being consistent, intensely interested in the work of the team, and projecting authenticity.

One way that we kept our teams from getting mired in all the potential office distractions—most of which are familiar to most companies, but a luxury that an organization in transformation cannot afford—was to become adopters of a Scrum approach. In fact, Luke and the team had introduced the methodology a year before I arrived. What we changed was to really embrace it where it made the best sense for us, and challenge and change it where it did not. We introduced project planning, metrics, an architecture forum, and many other enhancements. In other words, we made it our own.

Scrum team methodology is a hot topic in customer-focused DevOps technology development. Although the methodology has been around for some time, it is only now becoming fully utilized enterprise-wide for collaboratively solving complex problems. Scrum teams (scrum is not a technology term—think more about a rugby scrum than some insider acronym) meet every morning, not to talk about how to do stuff, but to make sure the teams understand what is expected and why.[18] Scrum presents a way to energize teams with a consistency- and positivity-reinforced experience.

GRATITUDE

We ask so much from the people who work with us. Yes, I'll reinforce *with* us, not *for* us. Their collective energy, honest feedback, and work make it possible to execute our strategies, and for the business to succeed. Undaunted leaders must realize that authentic gratitude and enthusiasm for the work of others not only creates a work environment where contributors feel acknowledged and valued but leads to more productivity and good outcomes for the business.

Alibaba Founder and CEO Jack Ma tells college students that "a good boss is better than a good company."[19] But Ma *seemed* to be projecting some form of gratitude onto employees, such that they should have an opportunity "to learn how to do things properly" in business. While it might be beneficial to find a leader who is willing "to discipline you, to train you, and to develop you," I'm not so sure that's why people stay at a company. It's probably your experience that employees leave a company more often because of a bad manager than because of financial uncertainties or product flops.

I believe fully that we all do our best work when we know that it matters. When our work is directed toward a common goal of the business or project, and we know that our peers will honestly

---

[18] According to the Scrum Institute™: a Scrum Team is a collection of individuals working together to deliver the requested and committed product increments. To work effectively it is important for a Scrum Team that everyone within the team follows a common goal. [www.scrum-institute.org/Scrum_Roles_The_Scrum_Team.php]

[19] "Jack Ma talks to De La Salle University students, Joey Concepcion in Manila," October 25, 2017, www.youtube.com/watch?v=3a-o7DqCu9lI

provide feedback and appreciate our contributions, we are all more engaged and productive. When they look you in the eyes and say, "I'm glad that you're here," those words have more meaning than any performance review or "good job" patronization.

I once held the Head of Research role for an amazing software company whose aim was to help its clients deliver new services quickly and cost-effectively. The company culture was fast, egalitarian, and exciting. We all had a mission and it just permeated everything we did. My group was tasked with developing the intellectual property and design principles and data models for the N+1 product release (N = current release; N+1 = next/future release). I was asked to not only contribute individually but lead the group who would set the future technology into motion. Our mission was set by a very collaborative, challenging, and grateful leader and friend who ran the R&D shop and who was also a founder.

My first tasks were to establish the charter for our team (which fortunately wasn't handed off to me, but was a collaborative effort with the Head of R&D), and to build a team of experts who could join me in this epic journey. We looked high and low and found some of the most talented thought leaders, software architects, and free thinkers the market had to offer. We established a few directions for the next release, and the one after, and then embarked on the collaboration of a lifetime. Half of these folks had advanced degrees from the finest universities across Europe and the US, and the others had likewise qualifications and many years of technology innovation and development.

We would work remotely for three weeks in home offices or at customers' locations and then one week a month we would descend upon headquarters like the collection of nerds and bearded weirdos (not all were male or with beards but those of us who did became the mascots for the team) we proudly were. While in the office, we would review the work and vigorously debate and discuss our findings and progress. We respected each other and everyone's contributions and gave back to each other real feedback and appreciation for their hard work. I still think back to those days fondly, and I am still friends with them all. We decided as a team that we would drive the intellectual property rights (IPR) creation together as well and so all the patents reflect that collaboration. I am named on several patents from this period of my career and the other inventors were like family.

Gratitude—*authentic* gratitude—built that team and made it exciting and uber-productive. This was a key element of the elusive magic-in-the-bottle that I experienced with this outstanding team.

If we look at the converse case, it's obvious that a lack of appreciation, feedback, review, and collaboration will almost surely not yield positive results. I have experienced a dearth of gratitude while on a project for a company that was moving into a new area, requiring a lot of context to be shared and learned, as we made a pivot of our portfolio. As expected, the information was complex, and the technologies and business conditions were foreign to many of the recipients of the work who would actually have to implement the technology roadmap. Initially, I saw this as resistance to our decided portfolio pivot. After taking time to talk with leaders and individual contributors to see why we weren't *feeling the love*, I learned that people were simply a bit lost on some of the context and topics but were afraid to ask questions or provide feedback that may make them look like they did not understand.

The culture had evolved to where once an expert had reached a level of credibility, they could not bear to risk the loss of their station in the eyes of the organization by appearing to be anything but an expert. It was all about "what have you done for me lately." While the transformation challenges were managed with some hands-on education, I had to climb a tall hill before I could create a community of interest for our new products and solutions. I had to demonstrate a commitment to our resident experts by helping them build the knowledge bridges they needed to cross in order to understand and appreciate the new markets we were entering.

A note on recognition versus acknowledgment: recognition implies "I see you," (I can recognize you in a crowd), while acknowledgment conveys that "I SEE you." I know it seems subtle, but the difference has a profound impact on demonstrating gratitude. Traditionally, we look to recognize employees for their hard work or contributions to meeting a strategic goal. We feel good when we throw someone a thousand bucks or plaque or a shout-out during an all-hands meeting. The employee takes their family on a nice weekend away and returns happily to start a new project.

But for the rest of the organization, we reinforce a culture where you must "prove yourself" every day. Perhaps that's the behavior that you are trying to incent, but is that a motivating factor anywhere else in your life? Are you a good parent because your kids expect you to be? That thought probably never crosses our mind. What we really want is that coffee mug that reads *World's Greatest Dad/Mom*: not because they recognize your hard work or your contributions to their goals in life, but because when they hand you that mug, they look you in the eye with the appreciation that their life wouldn't be the same without you. You make a difference, and they know it. They acknowledge you, for who you are, and acknowledge that you care. Even if you're "like a hundred years old or something," according to Peter's daughter.

VISION AND PURPOSE

A life lived without a vision and purpose is far less impactful, far less colorful, and I dare to say with less intention. The same is true for leadership. Making more money is not a purpose worthy of the precious hours of our limited days on this earth. And plotting a course to make more money is not the same as having a vision for yourself and your team or company. Making more money is an outcome from all that is in this book, running a solid and useful business that brings value to your customers, employees, and of course solid execution coupled with a little luck.

A vision is something very different and purpose hopefully brings *you* into the equation. While a vision may be for an industry, your purpose or that of your company is more personal and connected with what you can uniquely bring.

A vision starts out with a clear view of the present situation. This need not be constrained to the current offers in a market, as some of the most visionary inventions and businesses came out of a recognition of an unmet need. For this, there is no substitute for observation, research, and engagement with people/parties who participate in the market you aim to change.

Consider Apple and the now ubiquitous iPhone: Jobs and his teams did not invent the phone, the internet, the browser, the microprocessor, the idea of mobile communications, text, or any of that. They did have a vision, though, that putting all these things into a simple-to-use package would change the world. And it sure did! We all have stories today about how mobile technologies and the dramatically increased access to the internet has changed each of our lives. As we all struggle to figure out what is good, and not, from all of this access, we cannot deny that being able to see your family's smiles in FaceTime is just a better and more meaningful type of remote communication than our ancestors could have hoped for.

In many ways, a vision is a layered thing. We all need to have our own personal vision for our lives, we need a vision for work, and for leaders, you need a vision for your group, organization, or company. And for those of us who are called visionaries, we tend to have a vision for an even larger scope, such as our industry or society at large. The classifications don't matter here, the point is that your vision may be very personal or very grand in scope and that's okay. You just need one. And you need to be open to continuing the journey of self-discovery.

(For our purposes here, let's focus on a vision for an industry or market.) So, what makes a vision? Where does it come from and how do you know that it is valid or even feasible? It starts from your beliefs in *the art of the possible*, for a future that you want to see realized in action. This vision needs to be rooted in a clear point of view on the "good" or value your vision would deliver should it come to be. A vision comes from a recognition of an unmet need and an understanding of the situation and the potential benefits to your constituents that your vision would bring. Some visions may be grand in scale, while others may be far more modest.

Case in Point: A Vision for the Communications Industry

I have spent close to thirty years studying, contributing to, enabling, driving, and creating technology, business processes, and innovations for the telecommunications industry. I fundamentally recognize the immense social, societal, economic, and humanitarian benefits that telecommunications services provide, in all their forms, and have delivered to the progress of the world. I also recognize that the fundamental economics of these businesses are under pressure—they are losing relevance and share of wallet from their customers. While their costs remain constant or rising, their average revenue per user and profitability are on a steady decline. If they don't adapt, and soon, they may likely become essentially "utilities," and the pace of innovation that was their mainstay will dramatically slow, which would lead to a deceleration in the arc of progress we have all been driving, toward globalization, and the free and fair exchange of information and ideas.

My vision for the telecoms industry is thus:

I envision a communications marketplace where all parties in the supply and delivery of internet, communications, cloud, content, mobile, applications, and IoT, are all able to contribute their unique offers to a marketplace where consumers can mix and match capabilities that they need or want to pursue their interests. I envision a marketplace where the creation of these services is rapid, frictionless, and each party is fairly compensated for their contributions and value. Entirely new businesses would be able to form based on creating specialized bundles of these services, specifically targeted and tailored for the customers they aim to serve. In this way, I envision the concept of the mobile virtual network operator and enabler extending to all services, not just mobile, AND I envision that this ecosystem would include all the parties that are connected to the communications service providers, such as cloud and content providers. Today, these parties are combined in various ways via a complex collection of wholesale offers, web portals, distributors, and a hodgepodge of ordering and care systems, all isolated within siloed operations organizations with little to no context for the use intended by their end customer.

A vision is not a static thing, though. Think of a vision as a work in progress subject to revision as you learn more and test more. It's important to test your vision against the current reality: is it realistic, measurable, and attainable? We all recognize that the current reality is constantly subjected to change, and so the willingness and desire to constantly improve and challenge it will set you apart from those who may have a brilliant realization, but who miss the opportunity to realize it due to the changing conditions.

When you have a powerful vision and start to move to action, you will begin to see competitors and other actors start to sound the same and even attempt to take on your vision as their own. Fear not—your vigilance to constantly challenge and maintain the timeliness of your vision will enable you to maintain the thought leadership that led you to your initial and ever-changing vision. Of course, this is all predicated on the *actions* you take to move your vision from concept to reality.

A vision without action is interesting in and of itself, but ultimately not of much value unless paired with a powerful and actionable plan to bring it into existence. No matter how enlightened your vision, the market and competitors will change, and so must you. Many times, your plan may only address the part of the vision that you or your enterprise can drive or effect—that's perfectly fine and expected. The technologies and industries that shape the world today are complex and interdependent, and as such, no one player can drive an entire industry.

While this is true, it is not a reason to float within your industry: a vision will serve as your company's common view of your markets and the art of the possible you aim to achieve.

Be Who You Are

A life well lived may be measured in many ways, but perhaps the most important is the gifts we leave behind in the lives of those in our circle. The principles of fairness and level-dealing circumscribe our lives and relationships with friends and family. People often say, "It's just business" when they are facing some of the most challenging situations in our working lives. I vehemently disagree! We live out our lives and we make an impact within our families and within the lives of all whom we meet, work with, and work for.

The line between our business relationships and our private lives have all but disappeared. Sure, we must have some separation between our family time and working hours: but when we are leaders—when we lead others—the people enter our consciousness; we learn from them and indeed we impact them, too. So why would we have different principles for home and work?

We don't expect to be friends with all our teammates, but wouldn't it be great and more productive if we were? Our employees today yearn for coaches, not bosses. Coaches are respected as much for their principles as for the outcomes they drive. Both are important, but neither alone is sufficient to drive complex digital transformation programs.

As coworkers, managers, and leaders, we all face challenges and confrontations. How we choose to guide our behavior alone determines the impact we may have made, knowingly or not, on the lives of those around us. Our teams watch us all closely in both good times and in difficult ones. No matter the scale and scope of your digital transformation, my experience shows me that we must have a solid set of demonstrated and embodied principles in full view every day if we are to lead talented people through potentially the largest change the company may have ever undertaken.

"Do as I say, not as I do" never works. This chapter should allow you to say who you are and mean it. Your team will trust in the transformation vision, approach it creatively, work honestly and collaboratively and with a clearly understood purpose. If you never say the word "authentic" out loud ever again, I'm okay with that. You'll know it when you look in the mirror.

In the next chapters, we'll look at how to develop a vision that your team can embrace, and how to put your undaunted leadership principles into action to deliver on transformation.

PART II

CREATING A UNIQUE POINT OF VIEW AS A FOUNDATION FOR CHANGE

4

APPLYING PRINCIPLES TO DRIVE MEANINGFUL CHANGE

This chapter is meant to provide a practical representation and application of the leadership principles described in this book. Our objective in writing this content is to provide a set of real-life tested and workable models that you may apply within your business. Some of these concepts may be directly applicable, while others may require your own experimentation and iteration to fit the unique needs of your organization or digital transformation. Our hope is that this is the chapter that you read and re-read, that you challenge these concepts, write in the margins of the book, use what works and leave what does not. Our deepest hope for you is that you adopt a model of *progress over perfection* as you apply these concepts and drive your transformation.

Change is hard!

It probably sounds so obvious to say that change is hard, until you say it out loud. Say it with me: "Change is hard!" It seems like it shouldn't be, but it is. Resistance to change may vary from person to person, and organization to organization—complacency with the status quo, fear of the unknown, belief that failure is due to immutable forces, the hope for a technology panacea—but in nearly every case, the lack of motivation can be linked to a lack of a clear understanding for WHY a change is necessary. If the WHY comes from management consultants or three-day retreats or hockey-stick financial projections to fend off anxious boards of directors, you might as well save your transformation budget for hope-and-pray sales team incentives and president's award trips to Hawaii.

Instead, the WHY must come from YOU. You are unique. Your team is unique. The collective skills and experience of your organization are unique. Your competition can't replicate it. And an industry analyst most likely isn't going to tell you anything different than they will tell the next company they visit. Finding your WHY and turning it into a reality is a journey. And every journey needs a destination, a roadmap, a vision, and a strategy to guide the business as it executes and competes. Here's one we have tried and used effectively in our transformation challenges:

o The journey starts with the organizational acceptance that change requires a new destination built on the *art of the possible*. In Chapter 2, we seeded the idea of an organization needing a North Star: a vision of the future as it could be, with a strategy and a roadmap for where to go and how to successfully get there.

o The destination will be elusive without a committed **Owner**. Not a "driver" or a "champion" or a "sponsor." The Owner is the *lightning rod* for strategy quarrels. The owner is responsible for assembling the most strategic minds in the organization to curate the transformation journey.

o Before taking the first step, the team must admit that they "don't know what they don't know" (think back to the **humility** described in previous chapters). They must also admit that what they absolutely know to be true, may not be the truth as seen through the eyes of the customer/buyer, or the markets in which you play (that could include integrators, aggregators, platform ecosystems developers, etc.).

o The first step forward is actually a step sideways—turn to your left, turn to your right, and conduct your own primary **research** with customers, non-customers, former customers, end-users, inventors, app developers, service providers in similar industries, and futurists. See your industry with your own eyes. Listen to what's being said... and what's not.

o Create your own, unique **Points of View** (POV) on your marketplace. What's really going on today? Where is the buying power? Where is the flow of investment going? Which technologies are hype, and which are breakthrough? What would consumers do with that technology if given the chance?

o **Share** those Points of View with customers, analysts, business line owners. Debate them. Test them. Tear them apart. Revise them. Commit to them.

o Drive those Points of View into your **innovation** process. What market gaps could we fill? What market discontinuities can we solve for? What core competencies could we leverage? What new competencies need to be developed? Do you have "market/brand permission" to play in these areas? Would new products in these areas be strategic to your business and portfolio?

o Fill a pipeline with new product ideas. **Solicit ideas** from every corner of your organization. Create some ideation contests, with rules, screening processes, and communications that generate excitement around innovation. Create a process for shepherding new product/offer candidates through a filter of strategic intent and hurdles.

o Apply your informed business, technology, and talent judgment to identify and **prioritize** the most promising technologies—those that are most likely to impact or disrupt your business, systems, customers, and business model. Look for the big ideas in the sea of ingenuity.

o Foster strategic mindshare and transfer concepts into the **portfolio management** function. Advise. Consent. Iterate.

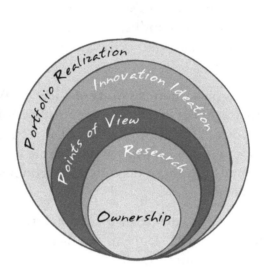

So as to not present this approach as an abstract discussion, we will attempt to apply the model to the topic of artificial intelligence at the end of this chapter.

TAKING OWNERSHIP

As the leader of this process, you own the accountability for creating a unique and clearly understood vision for the market and the organization's *wanted* position in that market. The Owner sets the starting point, the scope, and determines what "success looks like."

The Owner is accountable for assembling a team of analysts, strategists, and technologists that fully and wholeheartedly embrace the task of driving change which will have a material, strategic impact on the organization (i.e., an Innovation Team).

The Owner must pave the way for the team to move in and out of the various business units, provide the permission slips to engage with customers and public fora, and provide air cover if and when stakeholders in the organization begin to feel threatened and consider turning on their own.

For most transformation owners, the first question they ask of their team is "How will we keep this business relevant, as market forces, customer expectations, and technology innovations progress at an unprecedented rate?" In the course of the unintentional, but all too pervasive sub-optimization of many organizations, this question of relevance is lost. Product lifecycle management (PLM) driven business units are by nature ruled by incrementalism. We ask that of them. We ask them to execute on what is typically the embodiment of risk-averse business plans. "We *can* afford not to meet our growth numbers that no one really believed anyway; we *cannot* afford to lose money in a mature business."

We used to train consumers to think incrementally as well. Wasn't Caller ID such a neat feature? Now Grandma didn't need to keep a whistle on her phone stand as payback to telemarketers who were disturbing her suppertime. Intermittent windshield wipers were hailed as one of the greatest automotive inventions of the twentieth century. Those days are gone. Gone. It went out the window with brand loyalty, annual subscriptions, and *buying* music.

So, if the name of the game in the digital economy is relevance, and relevance is all in the eyes of the beholder, then all the more reason to take that task of seeking relevance out of the sole purview of the PLM organizations. They will know how to package and deliver the offers. But finding new value by scanning technology trends and taking notes at user group meetings is probably more likely to drive digital evolution than digital transformation.

The Perils of Innovation Versus Transformation

At this point in the twenty-first century, why are we still talking about the impact digital technology will have on the enterprise? Computers were invented long ago. The opportunities and challenges that computing technology brings should be old news. The difference now is that many enterprises who are trying to simply build a better (digitalized) mouse trap are facing an existential threat posed to them by competitors who are buggy whipping their business models altogether.

The business press likes to debate the difference between transformation and innovation. Innovation is typically related to a technology spark of some sort, while transformation is either some form of project management on steroids or a yet-to-be-defined concept. When it comes to driving change, we believe these two enablers cannot be viewed as somehow mutually exclusive:

o Transformation apart from innovation = strategy based on good intentions

o Innovation isolated from transformation = business value that lives in an intranet in PowerPoint that never sees an investment

Transformation not woven with innovation is like trading in your workhorse pickup truck for a Porsche with no gasoline in the engine. It looks fast and pretty in your garage, but you really wanted to cruise the mountain pass at breathtaking speed. Innovation that is dedicated to a research or technology organization often falls prey to the org-chart game of throwing the ball over the wall and hoping someone plays with it at some point.

DRIVING STRATEGIC, MEASURABLE CHANGE

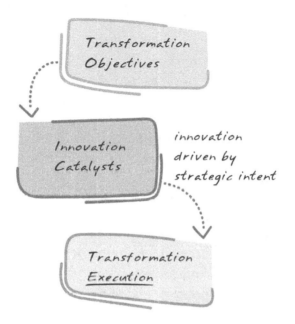

Instead, we argue that transformation and innovation must be clearly linked, ideally in the form of a single organization dedicated to the task of driving strategic, measurable change. This group would be responsible for making sure that innovation was driven out of strategic intent and will be utilized fully in the portfolio to drive economic value.

The Innovation and Transformation Office

While the mandate to innovate plagues many transformation owners, they shouldn't try to tackle these challenges alone or do so by solely trolling for part-time volunteers that contribute perspectives from various business units. While neither fully necessary nor appropriate for all organizations, a dedicated Transformation

& Innovation Office has proven, in my experience, to be a very effective and pivotal organizational model to drive meaningful strategic impact: from a mission statement, to envisioning a future state, to driving innovation and change in the business operating units.

A Transformation & Innovation Office is the Sherpa for your digital transformation journey—the sage guide who has scoped out various paths that can lead you through the rough terrain ahead to your digital destination. The innovation office (to simplify the reference) thinks outside of current planning windows, executions, and priorities. The innovation office lives outside the industry dogma, the failures of the past, and the dog-n-pony sales calls. Their task is to create value through vision and purpose. They understand why change is necessary and are tasked with bringing change to the business in the full context of both the current reality and the art of the possible future.

As organizations become mature, they can become convinced through the ever-present pressures of performance and measurement that their business model is safe. They intuit the industry trends and competitiveness through the sales channel and their win/loss rate for new business, their customer satisfaction survey results, and the accolades/ranking of market analysts. As a result, a virtuous but dangerous feedback loop evolves. The business can become blind to companies outside their lens on the market. The examples here are many and painful. Like the Bruce Woolley 1970's song, *Video Killed the Radio Star*...and then it all went digital!

Regardless of a company's choice to establish this office as an organizational function, someone, an owner, must take on this assessment and self-challenge as a disciplined task. The day your company feels secure and business is booming...look out! There are threats in the ether coming, and they are aiming to disrupt you. The most important part of starting a new business is to find a repeatable model of success, to find a problem worth solving, and then to deliver value against these mandates. A good shortcut, often taken by potential disruptors, is to simply find, study, and attack the weaknesses of the market leaders.

Disruptors find, study, and attack the weaknesses of the market leaders.

Every disciplined approach needs a framework. Below is one that has worked for us in the past: learn, think, challenge, create, execute, achieve.

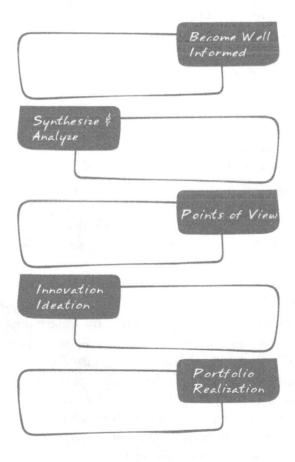

We will fill in this diagram as we go, step by step, then put it all together at the end of the chapter.

PRIMARY RESEARCH

Traditional market research is great. It is. It's a solid way to learn about new things and to stay abreast of your market. Given the intersectionality of business, technology, and society, we encourage you to know a little bit about as many topics as possible given the time constraints ahead of you. Day by day, the quantity and quality of market research improves to the point where no one has an excuse for market and commercial ignorance. While market research is valuable, you have to draw from many sources to ensure that your aperture is wide enough to see the space around your business and the dimensions of underlying fundamental transformation.

If your business has nothing to do with the migration of compute to the Cloud, you're likely missing something. Cloud is a fundamental and transformative enabler, and perhaps disruptive enough by itself to impact your business. The age of digital transformation is upon us all, and every business big or small is impacted, potentially driving, disrupting, and coping with technology. Even the smallest pizza shop has an eCommerce link to Grub Hub, takes Apple Pay, and is searchable via Google AdWords!

Having said that, conventional market research cannot be your principal source of intelligence for developing your vision for your business. Secondary research, information gathered by third parties on your behalf, is aptly named—secondary. It reflects the point of reference of the analyst, or journalist, or survey taker. Given their expertise on a subject, that perspective is fine for general knowledge, but it's not tailored to the mission of your business. Even when an analyst turns consultant, they often have an idea of the answer before the research project begins. It's not for lack of having your best interest in mind, it's sometimes too easy to let that which is deemed for the good of the industry to become your mission as well.

If you aren't sure of this position, ask yourself when the last time you heard an analyst look back in time and critique the accuracy of their hype-cycle predictions. By and large, it doesn't happen. Instead, hype cycles move from one to the next, in an evergreen process of finding the next shiny object or catchily-named technology trend. The reality is usually far less shocking, but potentially disrupting, nonetheless. Analysts can suffer from the need to be on the bleeding edge; the problem is this: just because a new technology is available, it rarely fully displaces the old, and if it does, it takes time and money. (Enter the CFO and the need for rational business decision-making.)

Change requires a compelling event—yes—and that event may be a disruptive technology or simply a disruptive new entrant; but if the study and strategy work is not done in advance, companies struggle to react in time, leaving them only the tried-and-true race to the (price) bottom at the expense of profit and future innovation.

One thing is certain in my experience in technology and transformation: You cannot *save* your way to success, and cutting prices as a strategy requires a degree of tolerance for unprofitable operations that few companies, investors, or CEOs can muster. Instead, you need to find a way to bring value, maybe incrementally for now as you milk that cash cow, but the cow will run out of milk and you need to plan for that day. It is coming, and your task is to go from strength to strength in your strategy, not from strength to loss of profitability, to near-death experience, the massive destruction of shareholder value, and hoping for a turnaround. No! You need to expect that your work will be disrupted, and you need to take it upon yourself to drive the markets and disrupt yourself and your competitors by knowing the world around you, and how to leverage it to delight your customers.

Even when you conduct proprietary market research, it's hard for the research house to engage the market through the lens of your business. Don't get me wrong, there are some amazing analysts out there, but don't try to drive fundamental change in your business by waving around a market research report at your business planning meetings. That is a tried and often failed strategy by the former Chief Strategy Officers of many companies. No, you need real, tactical, tangible, and relevant knowledge. You need to have an informed opinion and a clear set of points of view. If you want to move mountains, you need to bring inimitability and conviction to the table. Fortunately, you don't have to be a certified market researcher to find your unique truth; you just have to be genuinely curious.

An Investment in Curiosity

To seek your inimitable truth, you need to seek an audience with customers, prospective customers, former customers, partners, analysts, and influencers who are willing to engage in topics that might include at least the following:

o Strategic Road Map: what your company is investing in or evaluating and what, if any, value will be realized by the user

o Major Trends: a view of the market horizons as a context for your portfolio investments and roadmaps (including futureproofing)

o Strategic Intent: a test of the thought leadership that will be required to develop innovative solutions to challenges that cannot yet be fully articulated

Given the breadth of the discussion topics, you're plausibly looking at conducting dozens and dozens of conversations. The sample size required might feel a bit intimidating even. One of my innovation offices interviewed over one hundred and fifty C-level executives over the course of a year. The more diverse the pool of participants the better. Again, you don't know what you don't know, and you don't know where insights might be found. Strategic customers might have a vested interest in your success.

Disgruntled, former customers might be willing to share some brutal truths that you may never hear from your sales or delivery teams. Smaller, niche players might have their sights set on more flexible buying models (e.g., making expensive software systems more affordable via as-a-service models). And different geographies present sometimes vastly different consumer, competitive, and regulatory landscapes.

The investment in time and travel to meet with this widespread constituency is no doubt significant—commensurate, however, with the importance of the task at hand. There are some short-cuts available, so don't despair. For example, an innovation office can take full advantage of professional networking conference vendors. Unlike trade groups, these independent conference planners will pull together a handful of sponsors (usually leading products and services providers for a particular industry) and host a hand-picked collection of CXOs interested in a particular topic, such as a "Telecommunications CIO Summit." The delegates have their travel and lodging paid for (at some exotic location), and in return are asked to participate in peer-to-peer presentations and panels and required to attend private meetings with the summit sponsors (of mutual choosing), which we dubbed "executive speed dating."

We strongly recommend that you DO NOT let these primary research sessions turn into tacit sales or business development meetings. In fact, think long and hard about inviting sales reps to these discussions at all (or instruct them to be a fly on the wall). If the executive (customer or not) on the other side of the table catches the whiff of sales intent, they will stiffen up in their seat and go into a vendor-defense mode. Conversely, declaring at the outset of these meetings that your intent is research, with a promise *not* to promote product, will be well received—refreshingly so.

The goal is strategic alignment, some mindshare. You might be able to get permission from your Head of Sales to proceed (with cautions of RFPs in progress); you might not. Regardless, you need these engagements to form your points of view. There is no substitute for direct, honest, and open discussion on the most pressing matters of your industry with people who live them daily.

While these conversations are a bit open-ended (you won't know going in which concerns will be important to the person sitting across the table from you), it helps to have a common set of questions to ask each participant, so that you may assemble a database of comparable responses as part of your analysis later on. In our experience, asking for a reaction to a handful of key, overarching industry trends is a good way to get the participant talking. Participants often resonate with questions on how they manage their business:

o How do you measure your business performance? Across which key business processes do you operate and what are your areas of major concern or needed improvement?

o What is the relative financial impact of [one of your strategic portfolio capabilities or innovation idea] to your business?

o What are your key objectives that you have this year, and how do you plan to measure success?

o We have studied the potential impact of [a strategic technology] on your type of business; what impact do you see from [said technology]?

o We believe [express a relevant POV] likely relates to your company; does it?

o Who do you see as your traditional competitors? Who are the emerging competitors on your radar?

Given the open-ended nature of these conversations, we recommend that one person from your company asks the majority of the questions, while another acts as a scribe. It's distracting to the flow of the discussion for the interviewer to look away to a notepad. You'll want to capture as much of the details of the discussion as the format allows. The more detailed the notetaking, the greater the opportunity to weave thoughts together granularly, while collecting potential soundbites that will come in handy when it's time to convince your organization to embrace your vision. Though not your intent, you may end up capturing a sales lead—which means you may have to end up explaining to your sales team why you were meeting with "their" customers if you haven't done so already.

The responses you may get, from very simple, humble questions, may shock and surprise you. At one event we sponsored, we encountered a change-agent with a rather unique approach to quality. I started the conversation something like this:

We believe that your ability to serve your customers and retain your market leadership and relevance is likely directly impacted by your ability to effectively manage your operations center and empower your call center agents to increase the intimacy and engagement with your premium customers. How do you manage this critical success factor today? Do you have plans to change in the coming years? How will you measure the efficacy of your change plan?

The response we received still rings in my ears over ten years later....

Thanks for your considered and thoughtful questions. The reality today is that I know that my company needs to change, and I know that these factors would, as you say, if improved, drive real value and greater customer loyalty—but my operations leadership team is weak and complacent and so, I have implemented a process to wake them up. I read the national papers in the morning, and if my company is mentioned for a failure to properly serve a premium customer, I generally find the responsible regional head and I fire them in a public manner.

Wow! Just wow. That was unexpected, very honest, and yet an unfortunate answer.

On another occasion, I met with the Head of IT for a small communications business in Eastern Europe and the conversation went something like this:

We believe that your ability to optimize your CAPEX investment in new equipment could dramatically improve both the market perception of your business while enabling you to free up cash for additional investment in growth. What problems do you see ahead for your service and network transformation?

The response, with head in hands, was simply, *"I have so many problems!"*

Sometimes, people just need to vent. And that can be a great opportunity: to have meaningful engagement on how to address both the short-term critical issues facing the business while in the throes of transformation. But the most powerful feedback you can hope to receive may be as simple as this:

I am pleased that your organization has points of view that are relevant to my business and that you clearly understand the dynamics of the market and the competitive landscape that I face every day.

Interpreting Pain Points

Over the course of your research, you will become well versed in, and confident with, recounting your interview takeaways. For example:

o *The industry is concerned with huge investments required to meet the explosive growth in demand, without a clear ROI or associated revenue growth.* Or that,

o *Market uncertainties are stressing planning organizations without a clear solution. A legacy of bespoke systemization is screaming out now for IT consolidation.* Or that, o *Outsourcing pressures are driving a movement toward horizontal business models.*

And so on...

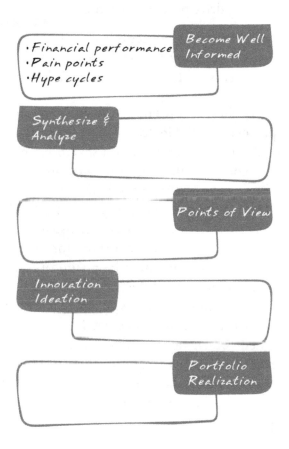

Identifying and articulating clear customer pain points may require you to put on your management consultant hat for a while. Some of the truths lie in what you hear explicitly, some may come from reading between the lines, and some may come from recognizing uncertainty when the research results are in conflict:

o The existing technology is insufficient to meet the users' needs, but the investment required to modernize will raise prices that will also harm the customer experience.

o Reducing staff saves OPEX but worsens time-to-revenue.

o Cost pressures are driving industry consolidation, but bespoke architectures and the lack of data hygiene typical in our industry, drive post-merger integration costs sky high.

o Incumbent growth strategies rely on expansion to adjacent markets, where innovative startups are set on disrupting the incumbents in their established market.

Like most of what we recommend in this chapter, research is an iterative process as well. Unclear or dichotomous observations may require additional interviews or a search for more obscure data sources. Expect conflicting opinions, and expect a high degree of ongoing refinement in your own understanding. The two things I learned for sure while pursuing my MBA are these: "One size rarely fits all"; and the answer is usually "it depends."

If you encounter completely contradictory feedback while your research progresses, this may be a sign of a needed view on market segmentation, the difference in business strategies of competitors, the difference in motivations of market players, or simply that the matter is yet to be decided in the court of business execution. When you encounter these occasions, fear not, there usually are real reasons for the discrepancy and knowing them can lead to a disruptive breakout for those able to understand and synthesize a solution that either brings them together or makes clear the obvious choice.

FORMING UNIQUE POINTS OF VIEW

Regardless of your research approach, there is no substitute for generating your own, deep understanding of your market(s). You need to understand your customers' wants, needs, and challenges, and perhaps your customers' customers and partners as well. I am *not* proposing that you respond directly, and simply do everything exactly how your customer prescribes. This was likely how BlackBerry lost its market leadership by holding fast to their customers' view that BYOD (bring your own device) behind the IT firewall would never happen. No disrespect to BlackBerry: I loved my BlackBerry, and still miss that keyboard, but the move to smartphones as consumer electronics platforms for apps just killed their business model. You will find that customers rarely can describe their desired solution, and even if they did, you would end up with a solution in your portfolio based on a risky sample size of a handful of individuals.

Instead, you have to be able to abstract the generality of the problem from your interactions. This ability to create an abstract understanding from a set of specific instances is a skill that takes some time and practice, but with experience, you can develop this and hone your ability. As an analogy, think of the case of two different types of artist: many artists attempt to capture a realistic image based on the subject they are focused on; by contrast, an abstract artist may see exactly the same subject and be able to create a model of that subject that expresses their perceptions of the *essence* of the subject while eliminating the image itself.

Regardless of your appreciation for abstract art, the process of doing this allows the future observer to understand the nature of the subject, while experiencing it in their own way. This type of thinking may provide the type of "Eureka" moment you are looking for when you meet with your potential representative customer groups.

Creating a point of view will also draw upon that curiosity factor detailed in the Research phase. To complement the direct experiences and information gathering sessions you performed, you also have to bring to the table your view on what's important to your industry, and what's not. In my case, I'm an expert in a number of areas because I have had many experiences that informed my industry perspective, but I have also studied adjacent and related industry challenges, and I am a student of technology trends and human nature. This may make me a bit of an egghead at times, but I'm always collecting information, thinking about it, challenging my understanding, and refining my point of view.

You might start by challenging that industry dogma—those "truths" about your markets that are still assumed to be valid—with respect now to digital transformation. I have known many people who lament that "all the big problems are already solved." This could not be farther from the truth! I see discontinuity and challenges all the time that would benefit from a new technical and commercial thinking.

Keep in mind that many times we convince ourselves that because a service or solution exists already, we should not try to create one of our own. Again, this type of thinking only serves to convince you to do nothing, to take no action. Uber existed, yet Lyft was still created. The market is big enough for more than one player many times. What you need to do is provide differentiated value, where even some slight or nuanced modification might be enough to wedge open a market (e.g., Lyft trying to appeal to younger riders). Creating your own industry points of view begins to identify those opportunities, or at least the starting point for a debate.

Keep reminding your team that where there are challenges, there are opportunities. Many great inventions and businesses come simply from the desire to solve our own problems—we are consumers as well as creators. As examples of this, think about the beginnings of the internet itself: to create a way for US Department of Defense researchers to communicate peer to peer, while not having to know much about one another or how they were connected. (We can all argue how this vision became a reality, but for sure the internet has dramatically changed the dynamic by which we communicate and gain access to products and services!) The inventors of Airbnb, Uber, and many other companies were trying to create a solution to a problem set that they knew well. Because they themselves wanted to use that new service.

We are consumers as well as creators.

Abstracting a trend in a business-to-business (B2B) setting might present a bit more of a challenge. For B2B, think more about the key business processes that you aim to impact or improve. You will be looking to abstract patterns across the instances of the challenges that you find in your research. Remember that at this point you are just trying to create a vision for your industry and provide a framework for discussing the major drivers and trends with internal stakeholders and industry "friendlies." The aim here is not to perfect a completely prescriptive narrative, but more to describe and present a point of view on the dynamics and expected trends that shape and drive your market—and then iterate, test, and iterate.

The Importance of Documentation

Given the amount of iteration of a point of view, it will become critical for you to regularly maintain sets of documentation of your points of view as they will likely evolve over time. The more detailed the better, as your POVs will be challenged (that's a good thing), and your intimacy with the market and facts will be needed in order to not only progress the debate, but to provide a platform to adjust your POVs as you add to your data sets and continue learning.

When organizing your POVs, consider your strategy and which areas you might expect to shape the dynamics of your industry. Let the data take you where it might, but at some point, you will need to weave the data into some common themes, so that you don't end up trying to "boil the ocean." Try to stay forward-looking, identifying gaps between the current state and your view of a future state, in areas such as:

o Technology Evolution:

- What are the technologies and business drivers in technology evolution?

- What are the main implications for your customers and the key opportunity areas for your organization?

o Competitive Landscape:

- What are the key new initiatives and programs around business efficiency?

- What are the new services being introduced?

- What are the new business models for delivering value to the consumer?

o Regulatory Changes:

- Industry regulation is at the same time a driver for competition and a source of endless uncertainty—can industry players still take advantage of change, or has regulation just become an impediment to investment?

- How does a vendor manage a global portfolio across the local/regional nature of the regulatory environment?

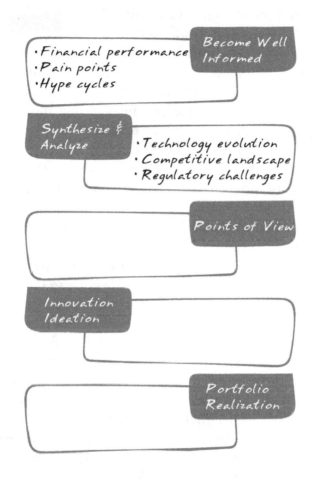

Synthesize & Analyze

At some point, you are playing a proverbial chess match with your data and insights. If technology moves one way, how will your customers react? If the user demands change, what will that mean to buying power in the industry? Every cup of coffee you pour will become a chance to build another If/Then scenario (if this, then that) across business models, technology, and processes.

When we applied this approach to telecom many years ago, we were in the middle of an industry that was facing margin pressure, with technology investment driving an endlessly high cost of doing business. Network technology was no longer a business differentiator, as all market participants could procure like technology at competitive prices. The communications consumer market was demanding real-time interactions, customized offers, and a personalized experience like the ones that they had come to expect from "webscale" service providers.

What we realized from our research was that the industry would need to move toward an era of *telecom awakening*: abandoning their proprietary architectures and recognizing that the desired customer experience could no longer be fully designed and implemented years ahead of time. Telecom services providers (aka carriers or operators) were looking for help with identifying the challenges on their critical path for which they could not fully define or articulate. They were struggling to reach out and grab future business and technology scenarios and pull them up close, to be examined and visualized so that they could begin to build their networks and operations toward those future solutions.

We believed that service providers would need to harness the power of their key business processes in order to maintain their service leadership positions and bring even greater value to their customers. They needed to design solutions that could accelerate the introduction of innovative new services and increase the service efficiencies required to monetize new assets and ideas and meet customer expectations. The carriers needed to reimagine themselves as a *platform* for a rich customer experience, lifestyle personas, and security, instead of merely a conduit of communications.

Of course, they needed to provide voice calling, text messaging, and broadband data services, but moreover, they needed to provide a mechanism for other parties to deliver high-quality experiences, while the carrier contributed its unique value in the combined offer. This was very foreign thinking for companies that had traditionally designed, engineered, manufactured, delivered, and assured every aspect of the service they offered.

They were also looking for a steady hand to help them through a time of extreme industry upheaval.

Putting Stakes in the Ground

What our customers needed was for us to help them *put stakes in the ground* on what the future could/would look like, the impact of market forces on their strategy and business plans, and what solutions they would need from us to help them achieve those goals. We needed to codify our points of view on the dynamic forces that were creating unprecedented uncertainty and competition in our industry.

We looked for: sources of differentiation, sources of disintermediation, sources of fundamental disruption, sources of inefficiency, and sources of value creation.

We had to know exactly where we stood that day, and then identify the gaps against our picture of the most likely future state, including:

o Technology evolution—the rate of change versus hype cycles

o IT and business hurdles that will need to be overcome for success

o Competitive threats and market disruptors—winners and losers

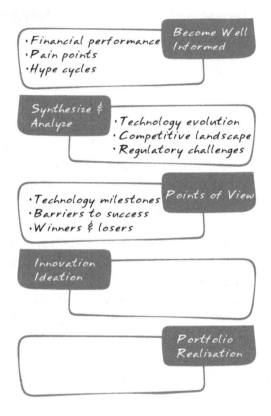

What would those *stakes in the ground* look like? Let's follow a line of analysis during the era of smartphone proliferation.

Milestones. As wonderful as the customer experience provided by the smartphone could be, the enhanced network demands wreaked a bit of havoc on the telecom industry. The economics crumbled. The existing 2G/3G network could not keep pace with mobile broadband demands, not at an associated sustainable cost, at least. The industry would have to embrace a network long-term evolution (LTE) that would bring existing GSM and CDMA standards into a single platform that would help drive down costs while delivering exponential advancements in speed and coverage, generation over generation. But homogeneity around a standard would fuel hyper-competition, with the separation of the service from the network being driven by both new entrants (e.g. Apple, Google) and by regulation (Skype over mobile networks), reducing the value of the network towards a utility for mobile data connectivity.

All-you-can-eat subscription plans would have to come under fire. Operators would have to withdraw such uncapped plans, all the while placing limits on the two to five percent of users that consumed a disproportionate amount of the total network bandwidth. Femtocells could relieve backhaul constraints and reduce churn for both mobile service providers as well as cable operators. A transition to IP would mean that closed devices would become open devices—a double-edged sword of enabling the opportunity to provide much-welcomed applications and services, but eliminating all barriers to entry from over-the-top providers—and now the last point of control for the operator to control the business case, would be placed in the hands of the consumer to decide what is and what is not valuable.

Hurdles. Telecom service providers would need to overcome technology complexity and seek massively greater efficiencies not only at the cell sites but within the access network. At the same time, margin pressures would continue to drive network sharing and consolidation, and greater efficiencies were expected. Differentiation from services would be critical for staying engaged with the customer base and not becoming a utility provider, driving the need to focus on service innovation and different ways in which people would pay for and obtain content.

Winners & Losers. Service quality and the ability to control customer churn in a saturated market would represent the biggest single risk to revenue, and a constant battle for share of wallet. The winners would likely be the providers who recognized that the consumer doesn't care about the technology that delivers their communications services, but the value of the applications they experience. The value game would be played by stretching for breakthrough automation and simplification of business processes.

Winning would also come from those providers who were able to let down their historical guard and seek new revenue sources in collaboration with content providers, end customers, and even their nemeses, over-the-top competitors.

We used these points of view to create several "value statements," which were a reflection of our organization's core beliefs, and the beginning of a storyline for how we needed to face our customers. Value statements would articulate how we would innovate by either: solving real-world problems with advanced solutions and services; providing the foundations of superior business performance; helping customers extend their service reach worldwide; and/or driving revenue by putting consumers in control.

The Red/Green Debate

The most energetic and fun part of this process may be the internal debate within your innovation team, or perhaps a product management group, that takes place before any offer concept is shared with the business unit or leadership colleagues. We created a *devil's advocate* game, which we dubbed the Red/Green debate, whereby we would split the team into two camps to debate each side of a point of view, as we sought to convert it into an innovation candidate. Since our team was versed in numerous technologies, we would draw red or green cards out of a hat, in order to remove any inherent bias from the debate.

It didn't matter whether you believed one side or the other yourself personally, it was the debate that mattered: tearing an idea to shreds before a stakeholder had the chance to do so at your demise, or at least professional embarrassment. In fact, we would often make the originator of the POV or innovation candidate take the opposite side in the debate of their insight, as they probably had studied the topic better than anyone else on the innovation team, but were too stuck in their pride-of-authorship to step back and question their logic for themselves.

The only rule was that whatever talking points that were discussed in the debate room—stayed in the debate room. For the gloves to come off, your colleagues couldn't hold any of your talking points in one debate against you, if you were to propose an opposite POV at a later date. This was an academic exercise, not a go-to-market platform. In fact, the random assignment game worked so well that we would use the Red/Green approach on our industry analysts' day, where we would invite the researchers and pundits to join along with us as we debated points of view on technology choices and market trends.

Not only did they seem to have fun debating their peers in a completely non-repercussive discussion, but we thought they may have looked a little more favorably on our organization, as we were highly interested in, and investing in, driving innovation and change in our industry.

5

CHANGE IS HARD

THE INNOVATION PROCESS

Yeah, that's right…innovation is a process. I think most commonly people believe that innovation is like a bolt of lightning from the sky or divine inspiration. Although some may be lucky enough to have such an epiphany, for most of us, we will need to conduct a thoughtful and informed, but iterative, process.

There is a really great body of work out there about the "design think-ing" approach, which I rely on myself frequently. This process is based on empa-thizing with a customer or representative set of customers to gain insight into their real needs and preferences. Once this step

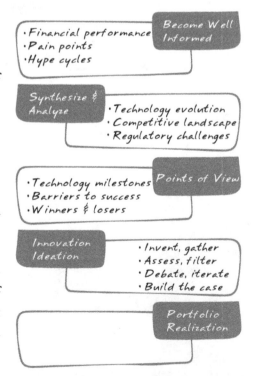

is done, we may be able to create a rough or "low resolution" prototype to share back with our customer representatives in order to gain feedback and refinement.

We intentionally keep the prototype rough, so the customer may feel comfortable to give us real, honest feedback. Think of it this way: if a painter shows you a landscape painting after they have finished it and framed it, and then asks your opinion on its accuracy, how likely are you going to be able to really tell them at that point that the painting doesn't really capture the majesty of the mountain range?

We naturally don't want to be overly critical, and we don't want to make people feel uncomfortable when we see that their work is in a finished or fully refined form. However, if I were to show you a mock-up of a graphical user interface (GUI) that I made out of colored construction paper, pens, and tape, you're going to be much more likely to tell me what you really think, and we may both have a bit of fun in the design process while creating a more user-friendly application.

While I admire and embrace this collaborative process, many times in the real world of business, we don't have the luxury of taking the preferred approach. You may not know anything about GUIs; you may not care. You may expect that you are paying me to know and to just build it properly. As discussed earlier, we have to do the work ourselves to a great extent, to understand the world around our business to be able to form a uniquely informed and uniquely valuable point of view.

Once we have debated our POV and we have come to some common beliefs, we need to test them with our customers and their proxies to ensure that we are in fact understanding their reality. In a way, this is the empathy step in design thinking but based on a pre-studied and thoughtful view of the potential problems the customer may have, based on our understanding of them and their environment.

Having an open-ended conversation with a C-level executive of your customer, without having a point of view, will likely ensure a short and one-time meeting. Senior leadership are busy folks, and they are looking themselves for how to accomplish their digital transformation objectives, which are increasingly vague and plagued by uncertainties. Asking these executives to talk about those problems, without bringing to the discussion any thought as to how you might begin to help them to address their challenges, becomes an exercise in your unilateral education—one that will end abruptly with a quick exit and maybe not even a handshake.

In order to solve a problem, you must really understand it, and problems today presented by digital transformation are many and complex. One of the major problems that frustrate progress is that the future is highly uncertain, and the rate of change appears to be accelerating without pause. This scenario makes it necessary to look for solutions that, while intimate with the problem space of your customers, are also inherently flexible and scalable.

We need to look to the pattern of our customers or our own challenges. If we may see the pattern, then we will more likely be able to create innovations and solutions that have the right "shape" to solve for both the pattern and the instances themselves. Pattern and shape may well be terms more akin to the arts, but as for myself, I see so much similarity to the skills and disciplines of both software architecture and that of a fine painter. The only difference is the subject, context, and tools. One may create a painting that surpasses even its creator's understanding or expectations and lives on as a masterpiece.

With respect to software platform architecture, sure the tools are very different, and the art may not be as readily appreciated, but it exists, nonetheless. The architecture of a digital transformation platform will either solve one problem, and thus become an extension to the sprawl of software solutions in the business, or it may be truly a platform built for speed, agility, extension, and digital *transformation!*

For example, let's say your company has consistently been underperforming in the area of customer service, and as a result, your customers have begun to leave you at a higher rate than is expected (i.e., churn rate). It's very tempting, in this environment, to look for a quick and dirty solution based on a not-fully-understood view of the real situation.

> *"Maybe we should just automate the call center and instrument it with a set of chatbots that can answer the most common questions."*

Maybe we should do this anyway, but without taking the time to assess, understand, and solve for the real problems, we are likely to miss the point and fail to deliver the needed change in experience, and thus the reversal of our customer churn problem. We need a *process* and not just a collection of reactions to issues that plague our business.

Innovation Ideation

We know that bad ideas somehow find their way to market. Unless you believe the marketing conspiracy theory, we can assume that "New Coke" got high marks from consumer focus groups before it was released. We also know that really good ideas often don't make it out of the lab or past a portfolio management committee. Most likely the innovation processes in play were not driven out of a market point of view, were not agile enough, or those in charge didn't fully know what questions to ask, or how to judge what was presented to them.

INNOVATION COLLABORATION MODEL

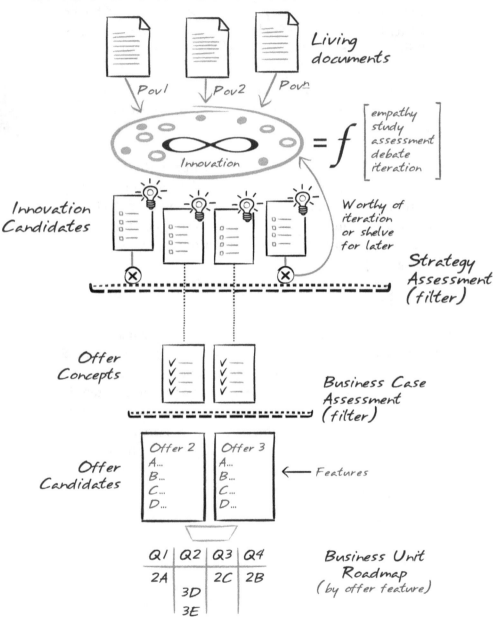

Innovation Candidates. Innovation *candidacy* is used to deconstruct the hype into revenue and cost. What is the market gap and why has it not yet been filled? Where is the spending in the market and what is the business justification/expectations? Will the savings in one area create a cost in another? Are their pain points addressable by your organization and do you have the market permission (brand, competencies, portfolio) to address them? How does this idea address your corporate and/or business unit strategies to change market positioning or perceptions (i.e., can you have an impact)?

Offer Concepts. In order to really take these ideas to the next step, you need to be able to create a uniform way to describe and express their value. A model that has worked well for me is the nine-question model, described below. If you can convincingly answer these questions in the affirmative, then you likely have a very valuable and viable new innovation that may not only enable you to progress toward your digital transformation but may also enable you to grow based on the merits of the innovation itself.

Nine-Question Conceptualization Model

1. What is it?

2. Who is this for?

3. What are its tangible benefits?

4. Why would anyone care?

5. What do you believe must or will happen (the POV that drives the need/adoption)?

6. What are the addressable markets and how big is the opportunity space?

7. Is this new or related to an existing idea/product/offer?

8. What is the indicative business case for your organization and your customers?

9. Who (which organization) would take the offer to market?

To be clear, the entirety of this exercise should be time-bound, lightweight (stressing progress over perfection), and iterative. Many times, I have used presentations or simple documents to answer these questions, sharing periodically along the way. This should not be a fifty-page document or a 100-slide presentation. This is an exercise in collective thinking, not a SmartArt contest! We just need to be clear enough to make our ideas understood, succinct enough that it can be shared easily, and compelling enough for colleagues to want to participate and iterate. Pictures, and now video as well, are truly worth a thousand words (aka, the pages and pages that most will likely not read anyway).

The objective is simple: to create a pipeline of innovation candidates that can be assessed quickly for inclusion into the transformation program. If the innovation is fundamental, then a leadership team may decide to create an entirely new business or offer, which would likely require much more additional due diligence and oversight as you progress. Regardless, starting this process, creating candidates, prioritizing them, and moving them into the flow of your normal business will be transformative by itself, and it will be a clear step in the ongoing progression of your digital transformation.

Describe It

This may sound obvious and it will definitely require some iteration, but we need to be able to truly describe in writing, prototype, and/or picture what our innovation is. If you can't describe it succinctly, there can be no common understanding, and therefore no substantive discussion on the opportunity, risk, and necessity of an innovation and its impact on our current or future phase of digital transformation. In describing it, you will likely find a lot of clarity yourself, as you think about how to explain it to someone else.

This first step in designing an offer concept can directly draw from the low-resolution prototype concept of a design thinking model. In many companies still, today, bringing in a prototype made of the same materials you played with in kindergarten would be unacceptable. The choice of medium for the expression of the idea will vary based on the company and its culture. That said, the need to clearly articulate what the innovation is, and what it does, is paramount to enrolling support, addressing challenges, soliciting constructive feedback, and marshaling the necessary iteration required.

This effort to succinctly describe the concept is fundamental to the process, as the rest of the offer development will build on either a solid, well-understood foundation or a mounting set of perplexing rationalizations and disjointed justifications.

If this task was easy, there would be a glut of new innovations in every company today. The reality is that it takes a lot of context and thought to be able to come up with and then describe an innovation. Putting forward an innovation can also be politically daunting in many companies, as you will inevitably run into the "we tried it, failed, and don't want to do so again" phenomenon, as discussed prior. Sometimes innovation is seen as a criticism of the current business or model of operations; it is this type of complacency and internal resistance to change that necessitates the type of transformational leadership and approaches discussed herein.

---

*Sometimes innovation is seen as a criticism of
the current business or model of operations.*

By clearly establishing an Innovation & Transformation Office, you are removing many of these hurdles to change, but some will still exist and must be managed through effecting solid communications, the execution of your process, making the innovation process accessible to the broader company, and celebrating the successes and failures of these projects. In doing so, you are setting the tone in the organization that innovation is not the responsibility of someone else. Make sure to communicate that everyone is encouraged to contribute (we don't know where that killer app is hiding), that there is an innovation process, that the ideation assessments will be transparent, that participants will be appreciated—and not punished—for calling out the need for an innovation, and that they may actually help drive the transformation of the company and its value creation.

Many companies have rewards established for innovation and IPR creation and run high-profile hackathons or companywide innovation contests. These are all good and necessary to incent participation.

What Point of View This Offer Is Related to and How

As discussed, having a point of view on the major customer problems, opportunities, the disruptions from competitors, and available technologies informs everything about an innovation. Innovation for the sake of it may be exciting and fun to drive, but innovation tied to an opportunity to disrupt, digitally transform, or to provide greater value for ourselves and our customers— these are the ones that create value and create the opportunity for growth.

Leave the incrementalism to the normal development and progression of the business lines or business units, should your company be organized as such. Incremental value is still valuable, but with a lower expected return perhaps, and lower potential risk. When considering incremental value creation, you still need to look to your points of view, though. Perhaps the incremental feature is going to become irrelevant to the business, because of a near-term disruption in technology, market, regulatory, competitors, or the like.

As an example, your research may lead you to believe that NoSQL database technology is a major disruptive technology that will enable companies like yours to process and manage vast amounts of customer data in near-real-time while providing for greater flexibility of operations at lower costs.[20] Your research has also informed you that your competitors, and the broader group of related companies that follow their business model and pattern of operations, are already experimenting with and contributing to this technology advancement. You, therefore, have formed a point of view that this technology is potentially disruptive, in general, and specifically has applicability and opportunity within your marketplace, and could accelerate your digital transformation ambitions.

Now, the innovation team is informed with this POV. They have assessed that this technology, indeed, could enable unprecedented increases in the speed and depth of intimacy the customer service organization could create with potential customers and have thus proposed an innovation to apply the NoSQL database technology to deliver on a new NoSQL AI-assisted digital customer service management application.

The linkage to the POV enables the company to understand the broader context of an innovation candidate while evaluating its potential impact before all the detailed assessment work is complete.

What Life Looked Like Before the Innovation

This question gets to the heart of being able to empathize with your customer, the potential user, or perhaps even the broader market. If you can put yourself in the day-in-the-life of the

---

[20] NoSQL databases are purpose built for specific data models and have flexible schemas for building modern applications. NoSQL databases are widely recognized for their ease of development, functionality, and performance at scale. They use a variety of data models, including document, graph, key-value, in-memory, and search. [www.aws.amazon.com/nosql]

"before" user, you can express their current reality and thus point to the real benefits the innovation may bring. If you cannot do this, then you likely don't fully understand the problem space.

For example, from a customer service scenario:

> Today customer service agents across our industry are tasked with both managing their customer's need for service in an ever-reducing call/experience time window while being measured on their incident close rate and product upsell per 100 calls. Agents have very limited information at their disposal, and as such regularly fail to meet the industry standard of fifteen minutes or less in complaint-to-resolution times. Furthermore, agents typically only drive a two percent product upsell metric because they don't have full access to the customer's service and support records, and typically don't even know the limitations of service usage their end-customer may have signed up for.

Do you see how having this perspective on the current situation allows us to frame our potentially disruptive innovations? This is a typical example in customer service organizations, by the way. Incident management systems do exist but are rarely aware of the historic customer data or product catalog of potential new offers. This, coupled with the advent of complex call center decision trees, usually deliver a customer to an agent predisposed to having a negative interaction, and thus the upsell is mostly lost before even attempted.

What Life Looks Like After the Innovation

With a clear description of the innovation, a solid view of the current situation and experiences of your customer, you may describe what the world of your customer or internal user will be like if this innovation were to come to fruition. This also allows you to iterate with your customer via a low-resolution prototype as you refine your innovation.

Let's look at another customer support example:

A customer contacts the customer support portal and is greeted by an AI-assisted agent application that has recognized the person on the other end of the chat, and has greeted them by name and prequalified that the interaction is real and with a real person. The AI agent requests a free text or video or voice interaction that enables it to assess the situation and either solve the problem or engage a live agent who has already been informed of the customer, the situation, their sentiment and mood, and has a few suggested solutions to try to work through. If the live agents are busy, the AI-assisted agent retains control of the conversation thread and updates the end customer periodically as to the support progress, or allows them to leave a callback number so the portal can route the next available live agent to them when ready.

Now that sounds like a much better customer experience that most people would recognize as valuable and differentiating!

The ROI for the Transformation and Key Business Metrics

By taking the time to quantify the benefits of the innovation (either internally or for your customer), you are able to express the expected outcomes in real terms. Benefits statements usually boil down to being able to provide some new strategic capability, progress toward the attainment of a strategic objective, the increase in productivity, the reduction of costs, and the like.

From our previous example, introducing a new AI-assisted customer service engagement application will allow our agents to resolve customer issues in fifty percent of the time, leading to an expected reduction in effort of $10 million per annum, while increasing upsell percentage by an expected ten points.

As your team becomes more proficient at generating new ideas and innovations, they will need to have a manner by which to evaluate the innovations to progress forward and in what order. You may well find that once you start this process, the number of potential innovations will grow quickly, or you may need to "prime the pump" by leading the process yourself for a few well-known issues or one of the strategic objectives from your digital transformation. Regardless, start the process straight away. The dynamics of today's competitive business environment rarely leave much time left to waste in idle contemplation.

The Competition for the Innovation

If the innovation is related to an offer your company would deliver as part of your product offer, the business will logically want and need to know if the innovation has competition and how the new idea may be differentiated from an existing offer. Although some markets are large enough to support many entrants, the customer will likely choose the offer that best suits their needs, and thus your ability to describe the innovation in those terms will help to differentiate it more than the always disappointing "it's cheaper" default value proposition.

Create the Indicative Business Case

This step will enable the leadership team or the line of business leadership to be able to understand the potential financial impact the innovation would have on their transformed operations, their cost of operations, or at a minimum, their budget. Many times, this step is overlooked or left to the team assigned to implement the innovation. This need not be a major financial exercise: it may be nothing more than a simple spreadsheet that models the high-level costs, benefits, and net effect on the business. If the business case won't come together on paper, or if the impacts are insignificant, the offer may get kicked back to the conceptual phase again for a new look (aka, iterate).

CANDIDATE CONCEPTUALIZATION

1	What is it?	• Napkin level description • Referencing your research, POVs
2	Who is this for?	• Customer, organization • User, persona
3	What are its tangible benefits?	• Metrics, KPIs • New experiences
4	Why would anyone care?	• What does life look like without it? • What would life look like with it?
5	What do you believe must or will happen (POV) to drive the need/adoption?		
6	What are the addressable markets and how big is the opportunity space?		
7	Is this new or related to an existing idea/product/offer?		
8	What is the indicative business case for your organization and your customers?		
9	Who (what org) would take the offer to market?		

Now that we have a model of a candidate conceptualization, it is very important not to spend too much time fussing with them, and it is important to make the process of creating them *iterative* and based on a refinement approach rather than a waterfall of perfection! Perfectionism is the enemy of rapid progress: if you have a top-five set of ideas, and you only know thirty percent of the information needed per innovation, that's okay! It's a good place to start and to use as a basis for refinement. You may well only be able to undertake the process of refining candidates one or two at a time.

By starting off with a few of the key questions, such as "Describe it" and "What are the key benefits and operational metrics," you may well have enough to get started. While we have proposed the full list of questions, you will need to assess for yourself if there is a more appropriate subset that makes better sense for your company. As we implored before, all the tools, strategies, and approaches presented herein are for you to start with and to refine, adjust, and fit to the circumstances of your business.

These innovation candidates need only be a short document, three to four pages with a low-resolution prototype and a simple spreadsheet. Making them perfect and fully complete will only serve to delay the progress and innovation the business requires. An overt attempt at perfection will also inhibit the feedback your customers and constituents will freely share, for fear of creating potential conflicts, misunderstandings, or reprisals.

MAKING JUDGMENTS

The end goal of a salesperson is to sell an instance of a solution; the end goal of an innovator/CTO is to create a solution that can serve as many customer situations and instances as possible within the investment and time envelope available. Again, the role of the CTO is more of an abstract artist, in my view. I look for the shape and pattern of a problem before I ever consider a solution or technology. Once I understand a problem at this level, I think of the *shape* of a solution that would fit the *pattern* of the problem, and so on. This **abstraction** allows for many parties to be able to contemplate the potential impact, as we refine our understanding from problem recognition to potential solution to market-ready offer.

We are all bombarded by technology innovations from across the information, communications, banking, transportation, and other knowledge-driven industries. We hear terms like cloud computing, infrastructure as a service, platform as a service, bitcoin, blockchain, 5G mobile networking, IoT, big data analytics, Hadoop, and so many others. We are in a time of unprecedented innovation and explosive growth in the applications of information technology. Every aspect of our lives has been altered in some way by these and many other technologies.

This environment, coupled with many robust open source projects that have yielded highly valuable implementations of many of these technologies into usable solutions components, has truly accelerated technology innovation. When cloud technologies are utilized, there are no longer any sustainable technology barriers to entry for innovators to develop and launch their business. All you need is a great idea, an understanding of your business model, some amazing software developers, and you could become the next Uber!

Not so fast…while the implementation and delivery technologies have become far more accessible to the masses of innovators, understanding your customers' problems, proposing a solution, and getting paid for it is still very difficult and elusive. That said, we *are* living in an amazing time of innovation, so this challenge *is* being met.

So how do we, as technology leaders, make the best decisions related to the business or commercial problems we aim to address, in order to create sustainable value for our businesses and its shareholders? How do we make the best technology selections that will yield the appropriate performance, price, and future-proofing of our products and projects? How do we decide who to hire, nurture, and promote to succeed us?

Obviously, there are many unique circumstances that should inform and govern any specific situation, but I have found a sort of "farmer's math" approach to these challenges in my own work day. I mean only respect by using the term "farmer's math," by the way. My family came from the farm, and I'll tell you this: a solid dose of common sense can go a long way even in the most complex technical decision-making challenges.[21]

The root of all solid decision-making is found in information, understanding, being able to imagine someone else's daily life or need (empathy), and the willingness to take an educated, risk-based decision. In other words, you must take action to be a great leader of any type, and in a rapidly changing technology transformation setting, this means you have to be willing to take risks and actions without full data and facts. This is not an excuse for lazy decision-making or indecision, but it is a mindset that favors action and progress over perfection.

Those who *act* can make use of first-mover advantage, and those who take too long waiting for all the risks to be identified, categorized, and mitigated, may simply miss the chance to compete or deliver the needed result to the business. Actions do have consequences though, and while many leaders claim that they embrace a fail-often-and-fast culture, *they rarely mean it*, and even less so do they create an environment where their employees have the option to experiment and contribute at their highest levels. We will talk more about that later.

If we break it down, there is absolutely no way possible for anyone to solve any problem of which they do not understand and empathize. As the complexity and the nuances of the problem space become larger and more diverse, the complexity of the solution will do so usually in a disproportionate manner—unless you have taken the time to really understand the problem space you are solving for, the rate of change expected in both the problem

---

[21] Did you ever notice how we have phrases that come from the farm life still in our daily lives? I remember this one my grandfather would say: "The corn should be knee high by the 4th of July." True! If you have enough days of water, sun, and have fertilized and kept the weeds out of your field, by the that point in the growing season your corn should be about 2½ to 3 feet tall. If you're not on this pace, you will have trouble and may not have a good crop year unless you act fast.

and solution requirement, the scale of the solution, and the like. In other words, you need to understand the problem in the abstract and its nuances as instances of your more abstract model.

As an example, the specific problem and resultant solution may be as follows:

> Customer service agents are not able to effectively provide support services and upsell customers with new offers because the agents do not have access to the customer billing system.

A specific solution may be then to integrate or connect the customer care and trouble management systems to the billing system, and thus enabling the customer service agents to have a greater understanding of the customer as they serve them. In contrast, the abstract problem statement and thus more generalized solution might then be described as such:

> Customers deserve and demand outstanding service. An outstanding customer interaction is defined as one where the agent meets the customer in an informed and context-rich interaction. That interaction is enabled by a 360-degree view of the customer, their service, their location, and their pattern of use over time.

A more generalized solution may be defined as: an information and analytics platform accessible by any customer-facing organization or representative, for the purpose of providing the information above, and more generally, any data source, enabling rich interactions and customer insights. We represent these systems in terms of big data analytics and AI platforms. The specific instance of this platform may well be to serve the billing systems data integration, but not in a one-off and point-to-point manner.

GREATER COMPLEXITY REQUIRES GREATER UNDERSTANDING

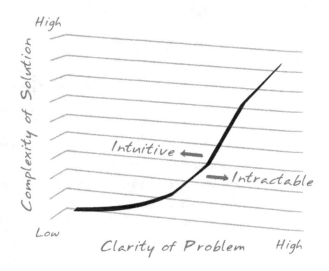

Many historic or legacy technology solutions have evolved over time, based on the incremental additions of capability. The pre-2000s technology did not lend itself well to the rate of change experienced today in business. This led to the development of "point solutions," or fully integrated systems that were stitched together with point-to-point integrations. These integrations led to additional capability, but also an increased long-term cost and a fragile infrastructure that became even more calcified over time.

Much can be said in this area, but the difference between today's modern IT platform technologies and the solutions delivered on top of them, versus that of tightly integrated legacy systems, represents a fundamental shift and improvement in the development of IT systems. It is this technology that allows unknown players to build amazing systems quickly, while the incumbents struggle to continue to offer their current solutions alongside their legacy solutions. If a technology-based company has been in business for more than ten years, I could almost guarantee you that it has a legacy application estate and that *those systems upon which they rely are now likely holding them back from their ambitions.*

In many cases, for long-standing enterprises, these systems can be thirty-plus years in production with limited or no change in capability or operations environment. The benefits of migrating the current system to a cloud-based compute infrastructure alone may bring much-needed enhancements to scale, while the applications may be refactored or redeveloped over time. Unfortunately, many times a legacy application simply cannot operate in a cloud due to technology limitations and the ever-churning progress of the IT industry.

CLOUD: TIPPING THE SCALES

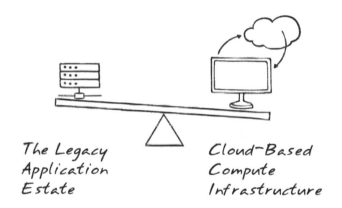

The Legacy Application Estate

Cloud-Based Compute Infrastructure

Although technology challenges exist and persist with legacy technology-based systems, over time they usually become highly efficient and tuned to express the business process of the enterprise they support. They truly express a full solution to a very well understood set of business problems and needs.

How did these systems become such a clear expression of the customer problem and solution set? These systems represent the collective understanding of the business built up over time by many IT analysts and business specialists. The system itself becomes the heart of the operation and as such takes on a life of its own. This approach was completely appropriate at a time when the technologies available were relatively expensive and limited by the computational power of their operating computers and operations systems.

As an example, think of the SABRE system running on VAX or Mainframe. This is the famed airline reservation system that agents have used for ages to book passengers on flights in the US. Although sophisticated in operations, the user experience is complex and based on significant agent knowledge and experience with special codes and control sequences.

Enterprises today simply do not have time to codify a rigid business process, and even if they did, it would likely become quickly outdated and thus prevent the required rate of innovation. Instead, an application built on an open computational platform approach is required and often taken. This allows the business to focus and build the application based on the needs of the end customer or internal business operations needs while utilizing an open platform for the more mundane, but critical aspects of their technology solution. Examples of this approach are seen frequently in the selection of database technologies, the adoption of cloud solution providers, and so many more.

The challenge again is that any business that has become successful will have a very hard time to disrupt themselves and will likewise be susceptible to external disruption.

"Disrupt yourself or be disrupted!" should be the mantra of all businesses. Even the most utilitarian business may improve their service or product or at least become even more efficient in delivering the value they seek to convey. Be very wary of the operations team or product management or innovation team who believe they have become as efficient and innovative as they can, given their circumstances. There is always, without exception, another party out there in the world trying to figure out how to disrupt the incumbent and break their business model.

A common strategy framework to consider is to give away what is free to you that may be core to your competitors. For example, in 2016, Wall Street kingpin Goldman Sachs began giving away its much-coveted software database, dubbed Securities DataBase, to customers. "The system represented Goldman's prime tool for measuring risk and analyzing the prices of securities," according to *The Wall Street Journal*.[22] Goldman sought to expose its competitive advantage of a cohesive, experiential database built organically over decades (whereas competitors had grown via fragmented mega-mergers), in return for the promise of superior customer loyalty.

Against this backdrop of forming your point of view and utilizing it as a mechanism to engage the market and grow your business, how do you decide what to invest in, and that which you should monitor or dismiss?

I look at this question from three perspectives in an interrelated manner as follows: business, technology, and people.

Business Value Judgment

After you have developed a set of points of view, you will start to see the many opportunities to solve the problems that exist in a business or industry. Your next challenge is determining which ones to solve and in what order. If you cannot identify a measurable business benefit for an enterprise organization in terms of real new sources of profit, reductions in cost, or acceleration of a strategic initiative, then you have no business justification to invest your company's time and treasure in this pursuit. You need to know, from the perspective of your buyer, *what's in it for them*. You need to be able to quantify these benefits in real terms and present them with a business model that they can use to justify their bet on you.

In a consumer business, you still have the same issue, but you may be giving value to a subscriber or participant in your service and

---

22   Justin Baer, "Goldman Sachs Has Started Giving Away Its Most Valuable Software," *The Wall Street Journal*, September 7, 2016, www.wsj.com/articles/goldman-sachs-has-started-giving-awa y-its-most-valuable-software-1473242401

paying for it by delivering real value to either yourself or another enterprise. Again, a good example of this is the advertisements we listen to on Spotify. They give the listener a free-feeling service and pay for it from the fees they collect from advertisers.

Technology Selection Judgment

But how do you make the right decisions and judgments as to which technologies to bet on in the development of your own products and projects? How do you make an accurate assessment? If you accept the premise that digital transformation is upon us all and all businesses, then, unfortunately, we all need to have or delegate the creation of a point of view on the evolution of the technologies that enable and drive our market's digital transformation.

I am not proposing that the CFO become a Python programmer or that the CEO start modeling complex data sets and developing algorithms in MATLAB. No, I am proposing that your CTO/CSO and innovation office form a point of view for your company and the related technologies that are most likely to impact or disrupt your business, systems, customers, and business model.

If you don't know what blockchain is all about and how that innovation may fundamentally affect the long-term chain of custody of user data, and that some smart kids in Silicon Valley are looking at your business and how to disrupt it...you likely have a problem in the making.

When I am scanning the market for technology trends, disruptions, and innovations, I use a simple model.

First, I look at the current applications of a given technology and compare that use with my POV on the industry in my current focus area. For example, there are striking similarities between utility companies and telecommunications companies in their operations, and so if big data and analytics technology is making its way into telecoms, chances are that the same would bring value unto energy production and distribution.

Next, I look at the implementations of the technology. Is there an open source project open and active on the technology? If so, how many contributors are involved and actively participating? Where are these developers coming from and which companies do they work for? If you find an active open source project with a set of diverse contributors in numerous industries—pay attention! This may be a leading indicator of a technical innovation that could benefit your organization in a fundamental or perhaps incremental manner.

If you have a software development team and your developers are talking about this technology and wanting to use it, listen and question the why and how. This too may be "I just want to work on cool stuff," or more likely it is recognition from your technology team that they see an application of the technology that could further your business objectives.

Finally, I look at the competitive technologies and ideas that are present in the market. This means that I have to maintain a broad awareness of many technologies, and have a point of view on the relative strengths and weaknesses of each. You have to ask yourself, as well, the "What-if" questions on the dependencies of these technologies. What if cloud computing as we know it becomes an edge/core hybrid distributed cloud, and as a result, the competition is likely to utilize this technology to create a service that is more attuned to "twitch" responsiveness, while my implementation of a database prevents me from doing the same should I need to?" Well, if you are at the point of decision on your next database selection, you may want to take this into consideration and design in this requirement.

On the other hand, if this is going to require you to build a far more complex solution that will cost twice as much, then you may need to just make this tradeoff and get on with it and implement without this capability, knowing the limitation and potential future refactoring of your software, its operating environment, or you may need to offer a completely new capability.

I recognize that this approach may sound too strict and potentially naïve. Agreed! Many times, companies and project teams build technologies on the basis of their bet of a future use that today does not exist. This is usually based on the inertia of an industry and its suppliers and providers of finished services.

A good example of this is the 5G network rollout for mobile operators. It was known that 5G would, somehow, someway, be built and deployed. The supplier side of the industry was busy building the technology required to deploy it regardless of end-consumer demand for services that require the specific characteristics of a 5G mobile network. The communications service providers will be rolling out 5G even before 5G handsets were available because they believed that their customers would build businesses and offers that require 5G. The thinking went something like this: We believe that eHealth and robotics-based laparoscopic surgery will grow at a massive rate, and thus our network must be able to support IoT applications with guaranteed no/low latency performance, and the market will be "big," so we will "find a way" to make money!

Although all this may be accepted as market truth, we technologists just have to accept that this inertia exists and that these types of massive changes will continue, regardless of the business case of the primary actors in that market. Some innovations become realities in this manner, while others must fight it out on the business justification alone.

People/Talent Judgment

The most complex and yet simple type of decision-making I am regularly faced with involves my team and how people work and collaborate. This book spends a lot of time on leadership principles and the approach for creating and managing a high-performing and engaged team. I look for the potent combination of talent, desire, and enthusiasm. I don't care where someone comes from—I care about what they do and where they are trying to go. I have had the absolute privilege to have many highly talented people in my teams ranging in education from DeVry to MIT. Each comes with their own perspectives and tools and has something unique to offer.

I, myself, come from humble beginnings and have done well, and so I expect that anyone can do well if they apply themselves and engage in their work with the perspective of a lifelong learner. I have, unfortunately, from time to time, had to let people go. But people make their own decisions, and if they choose to undermine transformation, or are uninterested in progress, excellence, teamwork, and innovation…they are gone quickly.

PORTFOLIO REALIZATION

Having a clear outside-in vetted strategy and knowing what to do and why is a big challenge and hopefully more clearly defined now by the approach presented in this chapter. As the business moves to a more innovation-led and transformation-led manner of working, it is crucial that the existing operating lines of business be intimately included and brought along in the journey to a more digital future state.

The lines of business exist for the pursuit of specific market-demanded offers, and as such, they are the customers of the innovations and transformations proposed. The lines of business are usually well versed in their customers' *current* reality but often benefit greatly from the strategy, points of view, innovations, and market engagement.

The separation of the lines of business from the Innovation & Transformation Office is obvious when viewed through the lens of incrementalism versus disruption. The transformation office is tasked with bringing needed challenges, innovative solutions, and model disruptions to the overall business before the competition, or in response to competition, and enabling the lines of business to take action and to implement change and new offers to remain or become more competitive.

In this way, the strategy may be more abstract and transformational, while the implementation may be more direct, vetted against the current operating realities, and therefore risk-reduced in its implementation. There are and have been times when a line of business is not transformed, but more left to operate into the sunset as its replacement is formed and nurtured. This, as well as so many other options, will depend on the specific nature of your business and market reality.

INNOVATION COLLABORATION MODEL

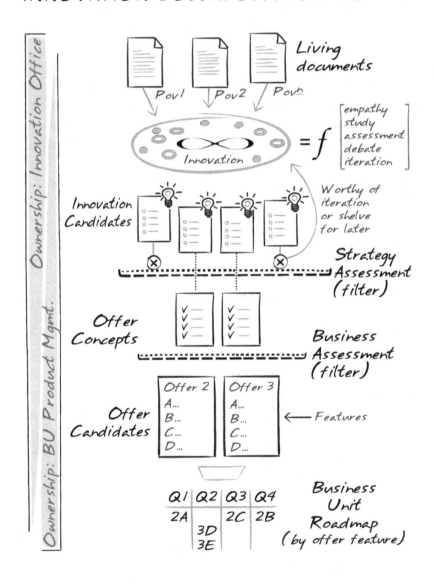

Creating and supporting offer candidates is where the proverbial "rubber meets the road." This is where the innovation office has to bridge the gap to the business unit for execution. The manner of this interaction may vary, but the concept is to create the points of view and gain alignment, or at least awareness of them, throughout the corporation. Some POVs will be more meaningful to one business unit than others, based on their remit and targets. Some POVs may well require an acquisition or the creation of an entirely new business unit.

Regardless, the consultation, iteration, improvement, and handover from the transformation office to the business unit for implementation is critical in driving a real, actionable result from the strategy work. This has been implemented in several ways in my personal experience, including:

o Regular meeting cadence between the line of business leaders, their Product Line Management/Operations, and the innovation team

o A phase-gated process based on the nine-question conceptualization model, and the refinement of the innovation

o Joint working via a seconded resource approach—loaning resources to the innovation office creates a greater sense of involvement and therefore business unit managers are less likely to undermine their trusted direct report

The goal is to communicate, consult, share freely, and jointly drive and refine the strategy through conception to implementation and measurement. No one likes to be told what to do, the same as "no one likes to be sold to," but we all like collaboration and most customers like to buy. If your collaboration is informed by a common market perception or POV(s), you have spoken to real customers and have their buy-in and/or challenge, and you are all incented on the same outcome of transforming the business; this model will not only work, but it will change the nature of the business itself.

If any of these preconditions are false—if the leaders are inauthentic, and the measurement of new innovations is too quick and strict—failure will follow. If we are going to fail at times, so be it! But let's not fail because we choose to not try or to not lead our teams through the uncertainties of a digital transformation.

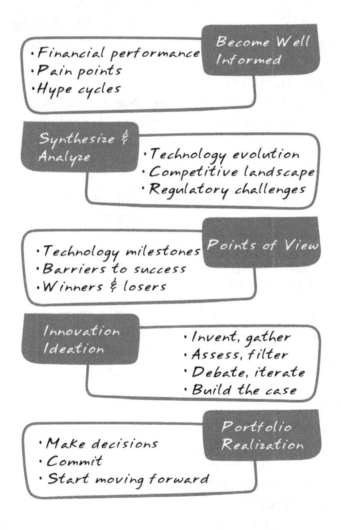

Realizing Change

After all the concepts presented in this chapter, we should return to the top of the discussion before we move on. The challenge we posed, remember: *Change!* Change is the hardest part of the journey ahead and to expect to undertake a change program as significant and potentially pervasive as a digital transformation without a clear organizational mandate, an owner, a process, and an operating organizational approach, significantly limits your chances for success.

The approach shared here has served us well in the pursuit of several transformation projects. Every organization is different and will require a more or less formal implementation of this approach. The purpose of sharing this approach is to introduce a set of tangible and implementable models and organizational structures. We strongly encourage you to take a systematic and deliberate method to your digital transformation.

Deciding to transform your business is significant in and of itself. It's a good and necessary start, but how will you accomplish the task? How will you decide what to do first and what initiatives, though interesting, will not be undertaken at all given other priorities and initiatives? How will you know that your transformational investments will deliver the type of experiences that will delight your customers and meaningfully improve the operations of your business?

Engaging the markets and customers in an agile and open manner will allow you to test your understanding and innovations in a risk reduced and lite-investment manner, while you focus the operating units of the business on the operations of their respective business, and hopefully, introduce radical transformations along the way.

Transformation is not a task, it is a continuous process of iteration and improvement driven by the tireless pursuit of your strategy, enabled by research, innovation, and market engagement.

Transformation is not a task, it is a continuous process of iteration and improvement driven by the tireless pursuit of your strategy, enabled by research, innovation, and market engagement.

6

ARTIFICIAL INTELLIGENCE
USE CASE

I n the previous chapter, we shared our methodology with hopefully enough depth for you to apply to your vision-setting.
As an added exercise, we thought it would be helpful to see
how this approach might work in your organization for a particular challenge: a decision on the impact and role of artificial
intelligence. Do your best not to get bogged down in data points
or the arguments that we will present. Rather, try to put yourself
into the conference room where the research will be compiled,
and the various points of view are analyzed and argued.

For the sake of this conversation, we will simply define artificial intelligence as a computer system simulation of cognitive
human behaviors. The game-changing, transformative nature of AI
rests in the notion that this software can learn and self-improve.
In some cases, it may even possess the ability to act autonomously.

So, with that as our backdrop, let's dive into our methodology…

As the CIO of "Incumbent Products & Services" (or IPS, a
B2B enterprise), your executive leadership team has begun to
worry that your multi-decade market leadership position could
be disrupted at any time. Revenues have begun to flatten, prices
are under pressure, and value creation in the market seems to
come only from industry consolidation. Your experience has
taught you that technology evolution in your industry has been

a primary driver of business model innovation, productivity, and yes, competition. You also have this feeling like IPS has, for the most part, done a great job at solving the known problems in your industry and for your customers. But you also feel that the next time a management consultant presents PowerPoint slides extolling Uber and Airbnb, you're just gonna lose it!

Instead, you preempt the discussion by asking the leadership team a simple question: "If we knew how to disrupt ourselves—how to upend the fundamental business model in our industry—could we do it? Could we execute on such a self-disruptive transformation? Do you believe that our company is susceptible to disruption at all? As the leaders of our business, how would you go about competing with us?"

If we knew how to disrupt ourselves, could we do it?

What you heard next was the sound of crickets. No response, other than everyone looking across the table, hoping someone might stand up to declare the affirmative. Instead, they turn to you and say, "Good questions—you should go figure it out. You're in charge. Thanks."

Fine—but you have one request from your colleagues: you want the privilege to pilfer their best and brightest strategic thinkers from each of their organizations. And you want to put them all into a new organization, an Innovation & Transformation Office, that has budget, authority, and leadership recognition. Okay, you need three things. And if we don't have the right people, we will need the authority to recruit them, but we will only do so if we all commit to listening and challenging ourselves to honestly undertake the work of this team.

While IPS has maintained its market leadership in terms of revenue and number of employees, it has lost its relevance in the marketplace. Younger consumers think poorly of the brand image, established channels are becoming more cooperative competition than brand advocates, and the brand doesn't carry over into any new market entry. Regulators treat you like a utility, with a level of compliance not imposed on the newer, more nimble players. And your CEO rarely gets asked to keynote at industry conferences anymore.

What IPS has going for it can be found in its vast amounts of data. You've got millions of customers, recording millions of transactions, and what seems like just as many customer complaints. You've tried for years to monetize that data, but with limited results. You moved what you could into the Cloud, partnered with a big data analytics firm, but struggled to hire enough data scientists to ask the right questions and extract actionable insights.

Searching for inspiration, you added even more travel to your already family-bending schedule, working in as many technology conferences as your calendar, and your spouse, can tolerate. When you return to the airport for your weekly dose of discomfort and bag of pretzels, the gate agents know you by name. You dined on buzzwords for breakfast, lunch, and dinner: The Internet of Things, blockchain, microservices, and artificial intelligence. Or was that machine learning? What was the difference again?

While sitting in the airport lounges between flights, fervently reading the *Wall Street Journal,* the *Harvard Business Review,* the Huffington Post, *The Economist,* and periodically looking at cat videos while listening to a toxic brew of heavy metal, punk, and country music, you come to the realization that what you are battling is a desperately-needed search for truth. A truth that now seems farther and farther away, due to all the noise of this digital age.

Now that your mind is buzzing, and the ever-present worries of your business come to the forefront, you would pen the same questions over and over again: How can these emerging technologies add value to IPS? To our products? To our customers? Are these even the right questions?

Information comes from so many sources. Which ones do you trust? Which ones do you believe? Your initial scan of the literature on predictions for the influence of artificial intelligence is all over the place. Research on the adoption and evolution of

AI quickly jumps to a discussion of singularity, when machines become as intelligent as humans, and transhumanism, where our brains become linked to machines. Ugh. How does this further our business planning and portfolio roadmaps? You've seen this kind of hype before, and in fact, you have many arrows lodged in your back from succumbing yourself to the panaceas posed by hot new technology solutions.

While scanning the web/literature, your innovation team sponsors several CIO networking summits: one in the Americas, one in Europe, and one in the Asia-Pacific region. The team surveys a number of customers and potential customers regarding their interests and commitments to AI. To cover the most ground quickly, the team splits up into several smaller groups but wants to make sure they collect similar information from their respective summits. Given the secondary research they have assembled so far, they develop a set of talking points that at least will get the conversations started off in the same direction.

Purpose of the Discussion

○ Mindshare on key industry trends

○ Chart the evolution of technologies in the hypecycle

○ Understand digital transformation goals and corresponding key business performance metrics

○ Seed long-term process and systems impacts and expected response from partners and vendors

IPS

Definition of Artificial Intelligence

○ What is your definition of AI?

○ How big an impact do you see AI having on our industry? On society?

○ In what time horizon? 1-5 years, 5-10 years, 10+ years?

○ What are the biggest hurdles, enablers, and constraints (regulatory)?

IPS

Priorities and Commitment

○ Where can you find discussions of AI in your organization (e.g., technical teams, innovation groups, customer-facing, C-suite)?

○ Are you investing today in AI?
  • Deferring/Watching?
  • Addressing in Strategy/Planning?
  • Integrating into Product/Innovation Roadmaps?

○ Are you organizing around AI? Dedicated resources, budgets?

IPS

Impact & Requirements

o What will be the impact on your business model(s)?

o On your portfolio?

o On your key business processes?

o On your resources and skill sets?

o On IT, software systems?

IPS

Your teams collate all the responses from your interviews, but their findings don't necessarily present a clear picture of the future of AI, particularly across the various market segments that you serve:

o Larger service providers are much more skeptical on AI

- Time horizons: 10-20 years

- Commitment: investigation stage

- Budget: thought leadership only

o Smaller service providers are "all-in" on AI

- Desperately seeking sources of disruption

- AI in all product roadmaps within 24 months

- Partnering discussions with platform providers

o Geographically: Asia-Pacific generally leading the way, seeking to "out-scale" the traditional market leadership in the West

The key takeaway was that IPS will need to consider whether to aggressively pursue the adoption of AI within its call centers and customer support centers, in order to reduce the cost of service, but those more nimble competitors will likely do so as well, with their inherent cost advantage. Your AI investment could be significant, so nailing down a concrete point of view will be crucial before sharing any concepts internally.

Your innovation team believes that they need to test the extremes, using the data points from your primary and secondary research. You lock your team in a room for the day, order in some lunch and plenty of coffee, and throw two thesis statements on the screen for them to consider:

RED/GREEN DEBATE

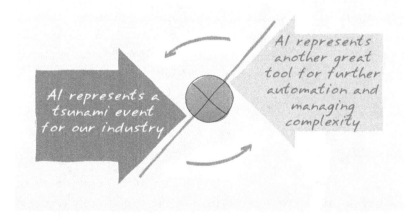

AI represents a tsunami event for our industry

AI represents another great tool for further automation and managing complexity

You instruct the team that the point of the debate is to identify and test all the potential pros and cons of the thesis statements and extract the best thinking out of the organization. You split the team into two random groups, break out a bunch of whiteboards and markers, and take turns challenging and defending each other's insights. The stakes are high, and your team will recognize and appreciate this fact and their fiduciary role in rigorously examining all the data at hand, as they form and express their opinions.

Your AI debate identifies some critical pros and cons for further analysis. On one hand, AI is being considered inside and outside your industry as a fundamental technology for disruption, and as such the major IT players (e.g., Amazon, Google, Microsoft) will invest heavily, and we at IPS will benefit by participating in such a sea change in customer care. Existing customers of IPS don't value your current, human-controlled customer service processes now anyway, and would most likely be most happy with a fully automated customer service environment.

Ultimately, if your competitors embrace AI fully, the potential for dramatically lower cost structures and resultant market pricing could represent an extinction scenario, with no opportunity to play market-follower catch-up.

The opposing position lays out a more managed and evolutionary scenario: AI isn't ready yet with any real systems today that support your go-to-market. Your operations are far too complex, and as a result, AI would be too expensive and sub-optimal for your real-world operations. True, that customers are already dissatisfied with your service, but AI will only make this worse by undermining the trust that your hands-on services brand represents.

Establishing Your Point of View

Let's say for the sake of this exercise that after weighing all the data and opinions, your team decides that to fall prey to the AI hype-cycle would be financially imprudent, and IPS should take a more linear approach to AI, as they would any other emerging technology like cloud computing or 5G networking. AI will have a role in helping to manage complexity and continue to drive automation, but in the end, there will continue to be a human hand at the helm of key customer-facing policy decisions.

You are confident in your point of view, but you also know that strategy setting isn't an exact science. Well, there *is* a lot of math involved, but try explaining your Monte Carlo simulation to your leadership team without them politely excusing themselves from the conference room to "take a customer call." Drawing upon our lessons from Chapter 4, you encourage your team to step back a bit from their strong opinions—channel their *humility*—and to seek out some feedback and input from internal stakeholders and key customers.

All this great thinking and analyses need to be documented for others in your organization to digest. Your colleagues also understand and appreciate that the "stakes are high" with such strategic positions. They won't accept being spoon-fed an opinion. They will want to understand how you got there. They will respond to the transparency in your proposal and research. They will respond to the empathy you have demonstrated with their customers and potential customers.

This empathy is the basis of what you are asking them to believe to be true, and that you believe will have a material impact on the competitiveness of their business, the competition for resources, their ability to market and sell, and perhaps their ability to stay relevant in their markets.

Your team creates a detailed, annotated presentation as a "walking around" document to take to every meeting they can schedule. You start them off with a template....

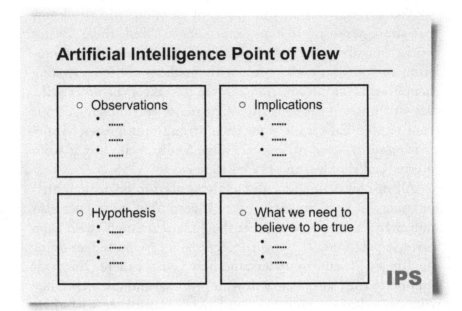

During the course of your vetting discussions, it becomes apparent that once some mindshare on your POV has been achieved, these meetings are also becoming natural opportunities to assess the impact of AI on each customer service process and begin to prioritize focal areas for AI in the business. Your team creates some graphical representations from their informal survey of your stakeholders.

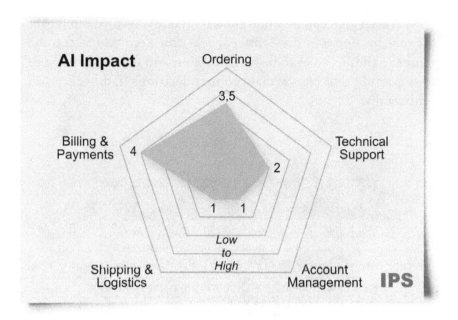

With this prioritization in hand, your team begins the work to populate an innovation pipeline. Employing your *making judgments* skills, you remind the team to make sure they are always considering the value equation: "How will our customers see the value of AI innovation in return for our significant technology investment?"

As the market gaps are reviewed, the innovation offer concepts begin to appear on your war room whiteboards:

o Chat Bots

o Virtual Assistants

o Zero-Click

o Voice Authentication

o Preference Prompts

o Personalized Offers & Discounts

o Agent Personality Matching

For each concept, an innovation template was filled out, again for socialization and fast-fail feedback. You decided to keep the template simple, so as to foster discussion and collaboration and to not imply that any formal product decisions had been taken unilaterally.

Offer Idea: ZERO-CLICK	
Description	Intuitive, zero-touch ordering based on customer profile and transaction history
Business Problem	% Orders left in cart rises with rate of SKUs
Differentiators	Customer database integrated across multiple lines of business
Solution Overview/Details	Predictive analytics module accessing favorites by location, time and context
Business Value	Every 1% cart-to-completion improvement represents $10 million per annum
Competition	Competitor zero-touch claims based on voice activation feature only
Customer Value	Convenience factor only
Level of Effort	2 - Moderate

IPS

Now armed with a great idea that fills a clear gap between your current process and customer expectations, you run not into the open arms of your product line teams, but into the proverbial brick wall. It's business planning season and the battle for budget in the coming fiscal year has everyone saying "NO." Or "Not invented here." Or "Great idea for the year after." Or "We've already got three proof of concepts running in customer sites where we're struggling to turn on all the promised features." Then your team starts to lose its momentum. Its motivation...a little. They worked so hard on this program, believe it's the right thing to do, but are mired in corporate frustration. "Change is hard," you tell them. "Change is very, very hard sometimes."

All this work now done, the level of conversation in the priority setting meetings is inevitably raised to the level of business decisions. Even if the budget is already allocated, do those investments and prior decisions still merit the support of the corporation, given what the team has now presented? Can the current initiatives answer *The 9 Questions* clearly? Is the culture now hungrier for facts and informed points of view over the previous, best-guess process?

I'm betting the answer to all the above questions is: Yes! If the most senior leadership has sponsored the transformation office, they will have known to expect some pivots and some controversy, as the organizational priorities of last year are now measured against a far more informed, empathetic, engaged, and yes even more analytical yardstick.

PART III

PUTTING THE PLAN INTO ACTION

7

EXCITING THE TEAM

In 1801, British polymath Thomas Young conducted a simple experiment on wave theory that over time has turned into one of the greatest conundrums of modern quantum physics. The now-infamous "double-slit" experiment demonstrated the duality of light and matter that exist both as waves and particles. In this experiment, a particle of matter, an atom, electron, or molecule, if shot through a barrier with two slits of similar size to the particle, would pass through the barrier and form a pattern on the other side not of a direct line that you would expect of a single shot through the slit, but of a wave pattern as if light or water had passed through.

What fascinates physicists is that when researchers set up an observation device, in order to see how one particle can interfere with itself to create a wave pattern, the matter then acts like a particle again. *The mere act of observation changes the behavior of matter at a quantum level.*

Now look up from your desk and picture your team assembled in a project kickoff conference room. How will they act if they think they are being *observed?* If they think you care? And how will they act if they don't?

WHY DOES OUR WORK MATTER?

Let's stay on that philosophical train for a bit. Why does our work matter? Why do we do the things we do, and why are so many of us willing to go the extra mile (or thousands of miles for those of us who travel extensively)? I would argue there exists at some quantum personal level, some set of fundamental behaviors that are motivated by observable, organizing forces, norms, culture, and expectations of the team and its leadership. There exists some organizational energy that can turn a collection of individuals into a team.

True excitement is like static energy. It's electric and you can feel it in the air when you enter a room or an office that has the "full potential charge." The challenge for you is to turn this potential energy into kinetic energy through your leadership and the actions of yourself and your team. The building of this excitement, and the replenishing of it, comes down to having a clearly defined and powerful vision that the leader and teams live every day. The leader cannot prescribe that "we are all to be excited today." No! The leader needs to *actually be excited*, and willing and able to transfer this excitement and vision to the team in a positive, productive, and low-loss manner.

Organizational energy is neither created nor destroyed. It just changes form. Indulging, if you will, my appropriation of the first law of thermodynamics: organizational energy will be either channeled for positive outcomes or it will find a ground in other ways. If you have a capable team which believes in a vision, but the leader does not model the behaviors, motivations, and is inauthentic, that energy is going to turn into friction, and the outcome will be a lot of heat in the form of politics, infighting, and ultimately failure.

In your career, I'm sure that you have experienced so many positive and negative examples of leadership types: the leader who means well, but can't help but fail to model their best self; the leader who leads from ego; the leader who just plain fails to lead; and then the ultimate hope of this book—the leader who knows what they want, has a vision, principles, and is able to conduct their energy and enthusiasm in a loss-free manner to their eager and continuously learning and improving team!

This is the model of the Undaunted Leader that we are aiming for. When this happens, the team takes on a life of its own and amplifies the energy, as their collective intention is aligned and joined to that of their leaders. The leader, in turn, gets more from the team than they could have ever expected or hoped for, and the results are limitless. That is what we are striving for here. That's the type of leadership required to create and lead a team through the many perils of digital disruption and transformation.

As a leader, have you ever thought about your own motivations and those of your team? If you have not, perhaps we can shed a bit of light on the matter from both the perspective of a leader and an employee. Neither of the authors is a trained therapist, but we have worked in, created, and led many high-performance teams through significant organizational upheavals.

First of all, credit to Abraham Maslow and his innovative model of the hierarchy of needs.[23] Maslow's model presents a perspective on human motivation that is clear to understand and has passed the test of time. In essence, if you're cold and hungry, it's almost impossible to care about much more. Once your baser needs are met, and you feel secure, then you are free to focus on higher levels and more abstract needs, like love, art, and enjoyment.

In my various leadership roles, I have learned about and tested many popular approaches to understanding the human condition. Many seemed to have failed so miserably, have proven unproductive and ineffective, that they are barely worth describing. That said, it's important to dissect some of the more common motivational approaches, in order to consider *what not to do*, as we look to a create a more humble and authentic approach to motivating and exciting high-performance teams.

---

[23] Abraham Maslow [1908-1970], *Motivation and Personality* (New York, Harper, 1954)

Deconstructing the Survival of the Fittest

We hear time and again about leading companies who systematically aim to "weed out" the under-performers each year, by strictly evaluating the individual's performance on some X by Y grid of model behaviors, rating them on some 1 to 5 scale, then stack-ranking all their employees against one another in determining their bonus payouts, performance plans, or termination.

This process can be highly unmotivating and often leads to unexpected and unwanted cultural outcomes. If you are a manager, you will need to spend an immense amount of time to go through this process, your HR team will likewise have a very high-stress role to play, and then you will have to hold meetings with each person reporting to you. The process often starts with asking each employee their point of view on their performance. I have found that many times the gap between your rating and their perception is wide.

Imagine, if you will, that you're a manager sitting in your office with an employee whom you have asked to rank themselves against such an arbitrary scale. Some will come in with "I am a 5 at everything," while others will do the calculus and try to give themselves a fairer rating in the hopes their humility will be rewarded. Inevitably, you will be forced to rank them on some bell curve, assigning a grade for a test of which the measures are typically highly subjective, where most of the students in the class will never graduate.

I really believe this process needs to be reconsidered in light of the need for constant risk-taking and innovation as most businesses face the daunting challenges presented by digital transformation. While you may be able to modify this process to be more fair and objective, in the end doing so will likely not yield a more highly performing team. I cannot recall a good meeting that came from this widely employed process. If you have a very high performer, and you want to give them fair feedback, maybe you rate an activity or two as 4 out of 5. Most high performers in the tech arena are highly analytical and so, they will ask you what could have made it a 5/5. Your answer will be subjective and difficult to substantiate, and likely only annoy them and leave them demotivated. Conversely, if you give them 5/5 on everything, but then proceed to give them a laundry list of stuff they need to work on, they will look at you like you're crazy! You just told them they are perfect in your eyes; now, you layer on this critique?

Suffice it to say, this process is not the reason why people create or find meaning in their work. The fear of judgment against an arbitrary scale alone gives reason for many to dread the entire process, and for the managers, they will spend a lot of time and yield little added value in doing so.

If the company policy is to cut the bottom X percent based on performance...look out! This culture will only reward the individual performance, stifle teamwork and creativity, and likely be rife with unproductive, innately competitive and tribal behaviors.

Additionally, many organizations expect managers to completely divorce the compensation/raise conversations from the performance review, and so will subject the employee to yet another demotivating engagement with their employer, after waiting weeks for that process to catch up. I have had the displeasure of being a party to many of these sessions, which usually go something like this: "Congrats, Tim. You have been evaluated as being an *exceeds expectations* employee, and your salary increase will be two percent next year."

Unfortunately, we may have all had to provide or endure this experience. I'm sure that you didn't like it, no matter which side of the table you were sitting on at the time. Certainly, it didn't impart any feelings of vision or trust or authenticity. Certainly, it didn't lay the foundation for promoting change or innovation. So, let's resolve to find a better way.

To be clear, the conversation about objectives, progress, and what's working and what's not, is all *valuable and appreciated*. The number mapping, stack ranking, and arguments about decimal points of progress are where this all falls apart.

The Murmuration

Have you ever seen a crowded sky in autumn, where massive flocks of starlings seem to dance in step to some silent symphony? I have, and it is one of those truly amazing and completely unpredictable phenomena, that once you have witnessed leaves you wondering why these creatures exhibit this behavior and where exactly they are going. These so-called murmurations can continue for minutes or hours, but each looks unique, organized in some way, and yet completely chaotic.

Scientists believe that this flocking behavior is motivated by a safety-in-numbers instinct against predators, creates social interactions, and provides a way to share information. While beautiful to observe in nature, this approach really made no sense in the way it was introduced to me in the context of business leadership.

I have worked for large companies who have considered this model as a form of leadership. The corporation spells out the vision, the leaders espouse it, and the "birds" (employees) will somehow naturally murmurate toward the objective. The potential of one bird is so much greater with their participation in an "inspired" dance of flight.

The problem is this: companies are made of people and people can see through carefully crafted corporate vision statements and marketing materials. Translating an extremely high-level objective down into an organization that needs to *do something* to achieve it is all but impossible, and generally does not ring true with the teams. Flocks of starlings would not survive very long if they were under the orchestration of one bird directing traffic from the back of the swarm.

It turns out that starling murmurations are actually choreographed by following a very simple, easily executed strategy: in order to evade predators through unpredictable flight, and without crashing into each other in midair, each individual bird only has to coordinate its change of direction with seven of its closest neighbors. That principle cascades across the flock (each bird will have its own seven), to which thousands of birds can evade a hawk attack with what researcher George F. Young describes as "the balance between group cohesiveness and individual effort."[24]

We need to recognize that a team is formed for a purpose, and while that purpose needs to support a corporate objective, the team needs its own, more tangible and realistic supportive vision and perspectives. Even though we may be part of a large corporation, we need to know that what we do is important, observable, and valued. The excitement around a vision for the team, therefore, needs to be close enough to the team to have any context of a feeling of contribution.

THE CONVERSATIONAL APPROACH

The conversational approach has legs: but be prepared to be authentic.

Conversations with employees without a sense of authentic self and leadership is like strategy without execution, as was cautioned by Sun Tzu. You're not just blowing smoke, but perhaps worse, your conversations may be rife with unexpected consequences, and wasted time for all.

"Strategy without tactics is the slowest route to victory. Tactics without strategy is the noise before defeat."

—Sun Tzu, *The Art of War*

Don't get me wrong: conversations are great! Of course, we need to be in a state of constant connection with our teams, where we are listening more than we are talking. These conversations should therefore not come as a surprise to anyone, and they

---

[24] Barbara J. King, "Video: Swooping Starlings In Murmuration," NPR, January 4, 2017, www.npr.org/sections/13.7/2017/01/04/506400719/video-swooping-starlings-in-murmuration

must be supported by a sense of purpose, spirit of transparency, and vision. Otherwise, they are just conversations that may be interesting but are likely not going to be focused enough to drive the organization forward.

This motivational approach really must be rooted in the leadership principles discussed in Chapter 3. Being honest, fair, open, authentic, positive, and consistent...all these principles must be on full display. Leaders can definitely take this approach and gain significant benefits from it, but they must be truly authentic in doing so.

One company I worked for decided to make a pivot to the conversational approach. They abandoned the tried-and-true but dubious approach of stack-ranking the employees. I really applauded them for doing so! The chosen approach instead was to instill a culture of conducting frequent conversations with our teams. Again, great! For myself though, as I started having these conversations with the leader I worked for, I realized that many times I was surprised by not only the tone and the message but by the inconsistency. Having conversations does not mean venting on or trying to manipulate your employees. It is a beautiful idea that can really drive amazing insights, teamwork, and productivity, but it can also quickly expose your leadership challenges. Conversation also does not mean simply telling your team what other people think or are saying. In the end, a team member wants to know what *you* think, and they hopefully feel comfortable enough to share their thoughts and perspective on how to create a great set of outcomes.

I Want to Know What YOU Think

I remember the worst leadership discussion I have ever had was in this context. I traveled to an offsite meeting to spend a few days with my leadership team and boss. The boss and I had a half an hour set aside to have one of these conversations; the topic was about the structure of our organization, post an acquisition, so I'm expecting that we will be discussing how we will move to implement the plan we have agreed. Instead, I was ambushed with his decision to take a different approach altogether, rather to discuss why his peers "did not get me sometimes," and why "some did not like me." When I pushed him as to where this was coming from, the answers were vague and completely unsatisfying, and certainly did not ring true in my experience at the company. After listening to this rant for several minutes, I felt compelled to interrupt the discussion with my bewilderment: "I frankly don't know where this is coming from; it does not ring true to me; and I don't care if people don't like me or get me; and if you cannot name these people and they are unwilling to even have a conversation with me, *so bloody what!* What do **you** think and what do **you** want from me?" I left that meeting feeling completely blindsided, unsupported, confused, angry, and fully considered leaving the company. I really do not think that my boss expected this at all. Looking back, I think he had made some dubious business judgment and decided to tell me this story in order to deflect the angst of his decision on me instead of facing up to it himself.

Rather than just walk out the door, I took solace in my work developing our corporate strategy. I felt that I had a solid relationship with the CEO and his reports to hold an honest conversation head-on with them about the transformation program.

The conversation with this CEO was open, transparent, and clear. He believed in me and valued my work, and recognized that the team my boss and I were leading and rebuilding was under a lot of pressure, and that much of the negative feedback attributed to me was in fact about my boss and his peers and their internal conflicts. I was unaware of the degree of tension that forming the new business had brought to the senior leadership team. His advice and encouragement were enough for me to put my thoughts of resignation away, and encouraged me to lead by example with my boss. We started having more productive conversations, and although I did not believe this situation was founded or fair, I moved forward with the work and were able to repair the damage done. Digital transformation is a complex, scary, and unpredictable fact of life. Comfort zones will be challenged;

some leaders will fight it and some will embrace it. Be ready for the rubber band to snap back a few times. It is always painful, but eventually, through persistence, communication, and embracing uncertainty head on it too can be achieved.

The point of this story is this: if you are going to lead intelligent, highly motivated people, you need to be authentic and tell the truth even when it is hard to do so. This truth needs to be consistent and delivered positively, even if the message is not what the recipient may want or had expected. You will be tested as a leader in every way when you undertake a conversational approach to leadership. Nothing is off the table for these conversations and a conversation is only valuable when two-way and truthful.

While I strongly advocate for this approach, the team who undertakes it must be vigilant and prepared for needed leadership growth.

Truly the Most Important Asset of the Company

It's all about the people...*yeah, right.*

First of all, the first part of this assertion is a fundamental statement of truth! In mathematical set theory, we would call this a tautology (of logic)—always true! Businesses are all about the people. A business exists because of some set of people who got together, maybe a very long time ago or maybe very recently, with the purpose of building something of value together! Great companies come from the confluence of great people with a common purpose, a point of view, dedication, and a willingness to strive for greatness together. Does this sound like your company or business? I sure hope so!

Unfortunately, the reality of people being the only real competitive advantage has become a trite catchphrase.

o "A company is only as good as its people."

o "You build a better company by building better people."

o "Our people are our greatest asset."

o "The people strategy is the business strategy."

o "Your people are your greatest customers."

Should I go on? It's okay to feel this way, but take caution: if you say it in front of your company, you need to mean it, and more importantly, behave like you do. This is the one area where you really cannot "fake it till you make it."

Long ago, when I first started out at Bell Labs in my first professional full-time job, I came to really believe and feel the reality of this fact. I worked in a group who were simply the best and brightest—yeah, there was a lot of formality at times, but there was also a deep respect and admiration among the people in the team that I had joined, that department, and the entire lab. It was truly a meritocracy. Again, nothing is perfect, and the labs definitely had some quirks and nuances to the culture, but I was proud to join and work alongside my teammates. I still look back at these days with warmth and fondness toward every single person. The questions I have considered for some time are why and how this culture came to be.

I think "the why" came from a joint understanding of the mission of the business and the mutual recognition that in order to have made it into those hallowed halls, you were automatically recognized as serious, capable, educated, and therefore were one of them from the start. The rules were fairly simple as well. This job was as much an honor as an opportunity, and it would most certainly be a palpable challenge. Given this, I wanted to do my very best every day to be worthy and to have that effort recognized by my team first and my manager a much distant second. The team would share freely (for the most part) and they would mentor, challenge, encourage and summon a sit-down if the youthful, newbie employees needed one. The people who became the technical stars were the ones who the team recognized as doing the work and solving the challenges together. Sure, there was a spread of performance, but it was generally skewed to the top.

Work and effort are valuable when they are valued.

Work and effort are valuable when they are valued. This became acutely obvious as a team member would be assigned a project with other people representing various technical areas of the products. There was an open and expected culture of review and collaboration. As a team member became more and more experienced and proficient, they would move on to more and more senior roles within these teams, and every contributing member of the team was expected to have their work reviewed by the others. The fact that the work would be reviewed, or at least read, made it valuable in itself. When I submitted a design or a segment of code or a new process, I knew that my peers would come to the review having read it with the sole intention to discuss it and how we may make it better. There were no criticisms in the feedback unless the person time and time again could simply not do the work. Although I never saw that personally, I'm sure that some people could not cut it and left, but the prevailing experience was of mutual and shared effort to accomplish a recognized valued set of objectives. For a time, the Labs embraced a more metrics and process-driven management style based on benchmarks et al. Even that wave of Malcolm Baldridge Project Quality Management could not dampen the drive and collaboration of Bell Labs...until it all ended for me in one day, with one encounter.

I think the year was 1994, and Bell Labs was under pressure as the move to become a more aggressively focused "commercial" company was underway.  The top leadership had reformed as Lucent, dropped our beloved AT&T "Death Star" logo for the Lucent "flaming ring of innovation," as some of us referred to it. The group's managers became more and more focused on the "metrics and processes" over the people, and to make matters worse, were no longer openly supporting the culture of innovation and sharing that had created the Labs. Performance review processes became even more formal, and as an employee, I started to feel more *measured* than *valued*. Sure, my teammates still hung together, but it was as if the leadership had moved to a different set of values, all the while professing their admiration and love of the people.

I started to feel more *measured* than *valued*.

One dark Monday in the fall of that year, the Labs called a mandatory department-wide meeting at the Indian Hill office where I had grown up. Our particular meeting was held in the auditorium, because of the sheer size of the organization. As we all settled into our seats, the normal chatter amongst peers was subdued and nervous, as the managers carefully walked up and down the rows and aisles of employees handing us each a white envelope with our names neatly typed on the front. As we started to open these letters, the department head started speaking to the group, reassuring us that each employee was being treated the same here, but that the Labs needed to make reductions in the teams because the financial realities of Lucent were more challenging than expected...yadda yadda yadda...then the gut punch:

> Your letter will inform you of one of two outcomes. Either your job is at risk, or your job is not at risk. If your job is at risk, this does not mean today is your last day, but that you will be speaking with your manager and HR later to discuss further....

As I looked at my letter, I was not at risk. Initially, I felt... relief? Maybe? But as my focus shifted back to the room, I noticed so many of the older and more experienced *giants* of our team were in shock and tears. Not all of them, but the numbers were really skewed toward that demographic. I was just devastated by this circumstance, and my entire affinity for this company was all but destroyed. The halls were quiet and, at least for me, something precious was killed and lost that day. I know many great people who remained, and I'm certain they continued the work with pride and honor—but as for myself, the trust was just gone.

Within a few weeks a scrappy little transport networking company a few miles away, Tellabs, was holding a job fair within the eyesight of Bell Labs. I walked into the place and up to a great leader named Anthony. I had never met him before, but he had a modest sign up that said "TITAN 5500 SONET" team. As I talked with Anthony, I told him I did not even know what all that meant, but that I could code like hell and loved to work in great teams solving difficult, important, and interesting problems. I had one evening of interviews and was offered a job to work for Anthony on the new team he was assembling.

As I went back to Bell Labs to inform my boss that I would be leaving them, I walked right past my office and up to the supervisor's desk with my resignation letter in hand. I expressed my gratitude for all they had taught me, but it was time for me to move on. He was shocked and dismayed and upset. He could not believe it. He told me, "Adan, you should have gotten the *retained* letter!"

All I could say was…"I did."

This story is shared here, of course, as a *what not to do* in how we express value and respect toward our staff. Now, as I'm a bit wiser and I have managed so many people over the years, I understand that sometimes job losses like my colleagues experienced are an unfortunate fact of our business lives. When this becomes necessary, compassion and care and true empathy are simply essential. These folks are not resources on your development plan… they are people…with families…with friends and peers among the team, and they must be treated with great respect. Beyond being simply the right thing to do—especially so if you believe that "it's all about the people"—should we not part with them in the manner in which we worked with them? To do otherwise will most assuredly cause great harm to your culture, and will likely lead to the unwanted loss of other employees you may be counting on. And if we ever consider the *giants* to be expendable because they may have the higher wages, or be more experienced, what are we saying to the rest of the company about what we value? You're saying to work hard, become the best, gain the respect of your peers, but in the end, you are completely expendable, replaceable, and should expect that someday will be of no use.

In Good Times and Bad

Do you believe it's all about the people? If so, then we must act like it in good times and in bad.

I've worked on many business acquisitions over the span of my career. We always seem to start off with a thesis on the value of a business based on some point of view we held and an admiration for their team and technology. That part of the process feels great and is hopeful for a positive outcome, should the acquisition consummate. No one rationally pursues a merger or acquisition to destroy value. But there is a darker reality as relates to the people. The euphemism for this is "synergies." Let me translate: this trope represents the people who will no longer be required because their positions are duplicative in the acquiring company. Many times, there are real and valuable synergies to be had, where the combination results in a value greater than the sum of the two parts, such as taking advantage of the scale of the acquiring company in their financial operations. That part may be inevitable, but how we treat the people in this process can set the tone for the entire transaction.

Firstly, I strongly recommend that you do your best to be honest, upfront, and clear to the company being acquired. As these people exit the company, we need to either negotiate their proper separation into the transaction or be prepared to do it right once the deal is completed. This can vary from offering a clear separation agreement, retaining outplacement services, allowing for internal transfers to open positions, and the like. Above all though, remind yourself to offer compassion and to be open about it. Doing this alone sends the message to the entire organization that "we do value the people," and that sentiment extends to the manner in which we separate from those who we can no longer keep on the payroll.

8

FROM SELF-DETERMINATION TO SELF-ACTUALIZATION

Most people will have at least heard of Abraham Maslow and his model of human motivations based on a hierarchy of needs, or have seen his adaptations of his model from *Motivation and Personality*, in the numerous attempts to explain humanity in various contexts ranging from politics to romance to marketing.

So, what does a book about human motivations from the 1950s have to do with exciting your team during a time of great disruption and digital transformation? The short answer is, well, everything. To illustrate the point, let's look at the model at a very high and non-academic level. Regardless of all the years of critique and criticisms, this model just "feels right" because it is generally true, and most people can recognize their own patterns of behavior in it.

THE HIERARCHY OF NEEDS

Please do not take this model too literally, and I implore you to not map this model to some extensive multipart project plan with metrics, controls, sprint reviews, and experiments. The point here is to think about the motivation of people and teams with this model in mind, but not too prescriptively.

If you apply this model to organizational behavioral science, then there is probably a PhD to be had for you in the future. As for myself, as a leader, I think of the organization as a collection of people, and those people are individual in their behaviors, with some common motivations, that if aligned, are far more powerful collectively in their actions.

Do you believe that actions come from motivations, and motivations come from needs? If yes, then this concept should make a lot of sense. If not, then I guess there will be other models to consider from psychology and organizational behavior to explore; but as for me, I'd say this is a fair approximation to start with.

I would prefer to assume that the physiological need aspects of the model are met prior to coming to work each day (i.e., air, water, food, sleep…). That said, never underestimate the power of free snacks on a Friday: a team that has the opportunity to share some goodies provided by a benevolent leadership team will create social bonds that are far more valuable than the small hit to your budget.

The remaining layers of interest in Maslow's model are as follows…[25]

Safety Needs

Safety refers to both physical and economic security. If a person cannot feel safe in their place of work or feels threatened in the security of their job, they will be far less able and willing to fully engage and contribute to the best intentions of your vision. In some companies, the culture of "weeding out the underperformers" actually creates a hyper-competition between employees who are supposed to be on the same team.

This idea of competition between team members comes from the feeling of scarcity for security in my view. If you tell the team that you are going to fire the bottom ten percent of performers, well then, you just created scarcity and unproductive competition.

---

[25]   Ibid.

You may still need to turn over part of your staff, but doing this in a manner aligned with individuals and their performance is far better and more productive than simply stating the "culling of the weak will happen in January."

Job safety is very important for some people more than others. I think that the lack of collective job safety, with the hope for wealth and growth, is, in fact, a highly motivating and bonding dynamic. For example, a company in startup mode is by definition a risky form of employment from a security point of view. We join these companies because we believe that we may achieve some form of significant and disproportionate wealth growth.

But for companies where the rewards are distributed to the faithful, who all share the same fate of success or failure, those cultures can be very dynamic and productive. Teamwork and contribution are simply part of the air that we breathe, and the flow of information serves as the lifeblood of the enterprise. That said, the same leadership principles still apply, especially when it comes to leading from participation in the work of the company and your group.

Teamwork and contribution are simply part of the air that we breathe, and the flow of information serves as the lifeblood of the enterprise.

As a leader, you must absolutely avoid, and not permit, the creation or promulgation of a culture of fear. Managers and leaders sometimes create this dynamic with intention. In this case, that person is not a leader, but more likely a bully driven by ego and the attainment of their own objectives over those of the organization. In this case, you will have to decide if this environment is tolerable for you as a leader, but in my personal experience, this can be managed through careful feedback and confrontation when required. Ultimately, no job is worth your health or happiness, and so I have no hard and fast rules here.

Leaders can also create this fearful dynamic though, without even intending to do so. This can happen because of a basic human understanding of authority and hierarchy. This is an old-school concept, so to speak, in contrast to the more naturally collaborative nature of millennials, as discussed previously; but it still exists. If a leader has a VP or SVP title, then they have some assumed degree of authority. This authority may be used to make decisions about not only the business but about the individual's employment and conditions of their work. Many times, through frustrations, callus language, unfair and unkind descriptions of people and circumstances, the leader signals that they are to be *feared* as well as respected.

For example, I once worked for a leader who would start off most conversations about how we needed to make some kind of change, by comparing and contrasting the current situation in a coarse and unfair manner: "Our sales teams do not know anything about [this or that], because they are a bunch of order takers who cannot sell value." Or, "that guy does not have a clue and is a real idiot." Try, "That offer is garbage, and no one in their right mind would invest in that." Ugh.

If you're an employee and you hear this directly or indirectly, would you feel comfortable enough to share your feedback or thoughts on controversial topics? Would you feel comfortable to make a case for a new idea or offer? Perhaps, but most likely not.

Leaders create a safe work environment where ideas may be shared freely and without the fear of reprisal. Furthermore, leaders are fair-minded and open to input just like any other member of their teams. Thoughtful, fact-based ideas are welcomed from all, and respect for all is the supported rule of conduct up and down the leadership hierarchy. Leaders must take extreme care and caution to eliminate the fear associated with hierarchy and coarse criticism. I am not advocating an environment without open respectful feedback and debate, and I'm not advocating an environment of tolerance for poor performance. *I am arguing that strong performance is supported by the elimination of irrational fear.* This alone will allow your team to move their motivations up to the next level.

Social Belonging

The workplace, whether physical or virtual, has a social requirement to it. How many hours do we all spend focused on the activities and responsibilities of our work commitments, tasks, meetings, projects, travel, etcetera? We spend all this time in pursuit of the goals of our employers, and hopefully, those goals align with our deeper interests and vision for ourselves.

While millennials have grown up super-connected, they actually have become by far more isolated in their social lives. The more we look into a screen, it seems the less we look outwardly toward the world and all the people that surround us. Our relationships with people are the most valuable and enlightening part of our working day, and yet we seem to be willing to reduce them to a text, an email, or an emoji. These phenomena are happening to us all, as our lives become more and more dominated by digital technology and working from home.

If we empower our employees to create real social connections, and collaboration is not only expected but prized, they will repay us in creativity and job satisfaction.

It turns out that humans are social beings after all, and they are actually far more productive when the work environment and culture recognizes this reality. If we empower our employees to create real social connections, and collaboration is not only expected but prized, they will repay us in creativity and job satisfaction.

If you don't believe me, just look at the rise of co-working and co-living businesses. Offices have given way to cubes, and cubes to open working environments. This dynamic is opposed by the work-from-home movement as companies aim to hire the most talented people they can, regardless of location. Even work-from-home these days has become more like *video-conference*-from-home, and it seems to be making a real difference.

The "how to achieve" step here is simple. Treat your team like you want to get to know them and spend time with them while you work. *The holiday party should not be killed off in your desire to control the budget.* The team-building event actually has a positive ROI. We need to strike the right balance between leadership and friendship. While a friend might avoid asking a person to take on a task that pushes them out of their comfort zones, a leader needs to be able to call on their team to do so frequently. The difference is a leader needs to provide the model for the organization they lead. If a leader is committed and takes on challenges and leads with integrity and technical excellence, the team will naturally follow. If a leader sees that a member of the team is not committed, they will remove that person for the good of the team, and if done in a professional and compassionate manner, the team will not only understand but may appreciate the willingness to do the hard things required to raise the overall level of the team. Competition for the best ideas and people is a real and palpable driving force in today's technology-driven, fast-paced work life. The best team wins! The role of a leader is to not only find the right individuals, but moreover create a team dynamic that breeds excellence, respect, drive, and excitement, all focused toward action!

---

*We need to strike the right balance
between leadership and friendship.*

It is a massive mistake to attempt to remove the friendship and collegial relationships from the work environment. People who have friendship for one another are not only better at working together, but they are also more likely to remain focused and committed to their mutual employers. Peter and I are a great example: the first time our paths crossed, I was in need of good people and I just saw something in him; Peter quickly recognized that such an act ran deeper than mere professional courtesy—there was a mutual understanding and thoughtfulness for a person, an individual, that you just happened to have met at work, instead of at school or a party. Add in some shared fates, killing time on the road, and swashbuckling stubborn product managers, and you start to care as much about the success of your colleague as your organization (though one leads to the other). Before you know it, you're writing a book together.

True friendship and collegial relationships are based on helping one another achieve their respective goals, in a supportive but challenging-when-necessary manner. I am not talking of "family" here. I am talking about friendship based on mutual respect, admiration, and a willingness to do your part to deliver on what you commit. How many friends do you keep in your life who *say* one thing and *do* another? I have *none*, over the long term. In my view of the world, a true friend will have your back when you need them, support you when they can, do what they say they are going to do, and encourage you to be your best. They will be comfortable in doing all these things because they are comfortable enough in their relationship with you that they may be honest and genuine every day.

I am not speaking of overly personal relationships being required or expected in the workplace, but I am certain that people who appreciate and know one another a bit are more happy and productive team members. I also believe that as a leader, we need our teams to know who we are and what our values are. We need to lead from a place of authenticity that is the highest expression of our true selves. We may be more understood if we are willing to share our stories and experiences freely.

It is not possible to be friends with everyone all the time. I am not professing a Pollyanna, tree-hugging form of leadership (though I do love trees and have no criticism for those who hug them!). Although we may not be best friends with our teams, we can be friendly, and we can be open and sharing our experiences, values, and points of view.

If you act as if you are above the team and that the members of your team are "other," you will not be able to truly motivate them. They may be motivated by their own objectives, and they may have some belief in your vision—but if you believe in your vision and want others to do so, then you need to be able to be vulnerable enough to let your team know you.

So, have pizza lunch on Wednesday, host Fruit Bowl Fridays, have an all-hands meeting that starts off with the team's special project to raise money for a beloved charity, while you video conference all your teammates doing time on the road. Have that festive holiday party...and...show up! Leave your ego at the door, sit among your team (not on some dais), and have some fun.

Esteem

Have you ever worked for a company that you were not proud of? We all can and should have pride in our work. Many people identify with their companies, areas of expertise, and the projects or teams on which they serve. Not only is this natural, but it's also a positive reinforcer to the team dynamics. Of course, work is only one facet of our lives, but for the working years of an individual's career, it is a considerable one.

People want, need, and deserve to be heard. This is just another one of those inescapable truths of humanity. Being heard in the context of our working lives, to me, directly relates to being valued as a team member, and having our work recognized on a real level and not just a superficial one. If a leader drives their team to produce some amazing result and never takes the time to read or understand the work, what message are they sending to those doing it? Although perhaps unintentional, the message is clear, it's the message of *otherness*. "You do the work; that's your job; my job is to manage you to get the result." On the other hand, if a work product is created, and the author is granted a few minutes to share the solution at the next sprint review, and perhaps even at the next all-hands, assuming it's sufficiently significant, then the team will benefit from some understanding, and the team member may be better understood and feel more appreciated.

Frame of reference

Having many amazing artists in my life perhaps gives me this point of view as well: the work of a painter is so much more fulfilling to them when it is viewed by others. When you stand back, squint a little bit, and peer into that moment or perspective of someone else, you learn something about them. If you observe carefully, you may see how they hold and use their brush, or you may see their preferences for colors and techniques of interpretation. And in the case of a modern artist, you may understand the power of their perspective to create an abstraction of reality that says something altogether different than the original inspiration.

Today's technologies are so significantly complex and comprehensive that utilizing them is as much an art as it is a matter of disciplined engineering. We expect engineering to be appreciated for its intrinsic values alone: speed, performance, fit for purpose, etcetera. Yet, when you consider the literally thousands of decisions that are made in the creation of a painting or work of art, we consider this a gift, or some conferred perspective learned through training and apprenticeship. It is! More importantly, we view and hopefully appreciate it for what it is...*art!* Art is the creative and skilled effort to synthesize something unique from the materials and experiences we uniquely possess. This is exactly the same type of process that a talented software developer or engineer employs to create an elegant solution to a set of problems.

There is art in everything we do and if we believed that, and appreciated our team as if they were artists instead of resources, we would find a way to create and foster an environment where they may not only be understood more fully but may experience some degree of esteem from their peers no matter what discipline they may work in.

Self-Actualization

I could write a whole book on the topic of self-actualization, but in the context of this chapter, I have but one thought to share: self-actualized people are leading their best lives doing fulfilling work, and have their intentions aligned with their actions. The lines between work and home have been blurring for a long time, and as such, it is a necessity that we, as leaders, not only aim to be self-actualized in our lives but that we provide the basic underpinnings in our companies so that our teams may hope to reach their full personal and professional potential.

Self-actualized people are leading their best lives doing fulfilling work, and have their intentions aligned with their actions.

Maslow pointed to US President Abraham Lincoln as having achieved self-actualization later in life, after the trials of waging a civil war. Lincoln's self-actualization was codified perhaps, in his infamous "Gettysburg Address." On the nineteenth of November of 1863, President Lincoln delivered a powerful yet succinct speech, *using just 272 words* at the dedication ceremony for a new national cemetery. That address not only captured his station in life but conserved the freedoms inherent in the American experience.

FOURSCORE AND SEVEN YEARS AGO OUR FATHERS BROUGHT FORTH ON THIS CONTINENT, A NEW NATION, CONCEIVED IN LIBERTY, AND DEDICATED TO THE PROPOSITION THAT ALL MEN ARE CREATED EQUAL.

NOW WE ARE ENGAGED IN A GREAT CIVIL WAR, TESTING WHETHER THAT NATION, OR ANY NATION SO CONCEIVED AND SO DEDICATED, CAN LONG ENDURE. WE ARE MET ON A GREAT BATTLE-FIELD OF THAT WAR. WE HAVE COME TO DEDICATE A PORTION OF THAT FIELD, AS A FINAL RESTING PLACE FOR THOSE WHO HERE GAVE THEIR LIVES THAT THAT NATION MIGHT LIVE. IT IS ALTOGETHER FITTING AND PROPER THAT WE SHOULD DO THIS.

BUT, IN A LARGER SENSE, WE CANNOT DEDICATE—WE CANNOT CONSECRATE—WE CANNOT HALLOW—THIS GROUND. THE BRAVE MEN, LIVING AND DEAD, WHO STRUGGLED HERE, HAVE CONSECRATED IT, FAR ABOVE OUR POOR POWER TO ADD OR DETRACT.

THE WORLD WILL LITTLE NOTE, NOR LONG REMEMBER WHAT WE SAY HERE, BUT IT CAN NEVER FORGET WHAT THEY DID HERE. IT IS FOR US THE LIVING, RATHER, TO BE DEDICATED HERE TO THE UNFINISHED WORK WHICH THEY WHO FOUGHT HERE HAVE THUS FAR SO NOBLY ADVANCED. IT IS RATHER FOR US TO BE HERE DEDICATED TO THE GREAT TASK REMAINING BEFORE US—THAT FROM THESE HONORED DEAD WE TAKE INCREASED DEVOTION TO THAT CAUSE FOR WHICH THEY GAVE THE LAST FULL MEASURE OF DEVOTION—THAT WE HERE HIGHLY RESOLVE THAT THESE DEAD SHALL NOT HAVE DIED IN VAIN—THAT THIS NATION, UNDER GOD, SHALL HAVE A NEW BIRTH OF FREEDOM—AND THAT GOVERNMENT OF THE PEOPLE, BY THE PEOPLE, FOR THE PEOPLE, SHALL NOT PERISH FROM THE EARTH.

Lincoln remains the most significant and pervasive role model for my personal brand of leadership. His clarity of thought, willingness to build the best team he could, his principles, and his commitment to a vision still speak to me personally and dare I say...to us all.

Channeling Your Inner William Wallace

Leaders have to *lead*, not only manage. The leadership approaches of yesterday belong there, in the bygones. Excitement is like static energy, and it will find a form of kinetic release either for the good or bad. In order to excite and motivate the team, we need to create and live our vision while working among the team. We need to recognize that we all have a story, and all have our goals, but there is great commonality in motivations.

Authentic leaders are best able to lead when they are secure enough to share their values and stories and are open and honest enough to accept that we all have a lot to learn, and as such, conversations are two-way, honest, and frequent. The challenge to convey authenticity cannot be underestimated, but your views expressed must be fair and free of the views of others. A team will cross the field of battle for a leader who is with them on the days of the contest, and who has their backs, while encouraging them to do their very best, by showing them how to do so via example.

In the 1995 motion picture *Braveheart,* the protagonist Sir William Wallace, a resistance leader during the wars for Scottish independence, needed to motivate a rag-tag army to fight to the death for their freedom from the rule of the English monarchy at the battle at Stirling. In the first line of his rallying cry, the Wallace character declares only this:

"Sons of Scotland, I am William Wallace."

No self-aggrandizements. No delusions of grandeur. No accolades. Just his authentic self. I am who I am.

PICK UP THE PEN

Writing on a whiteboard takes guts, but it really shouldn't have to. Every imaginable, scary aspect of public speaking comes into full view when you are asked to stand in front of a blank board and begin trying to express in real time your abstract ideas in a semi-tangible manner. Your writing, spelling, organization, and drawing skills are all on full display for everyone to see. For me, it's second nature, as I have been well conditioned from all the years of technical collaboration and design to do just this. A picture is indeed worth a thousand words! A picture allows the room to grab onto a model of something being communicated in a more specific manner.

I have noticed that this approach seems to be second nature for my engineering colleagues as well. As the complexity of a topic increases, we all struggle with the need to create an abstract model of it. This model allows us to focus on the most important aspects while allowing the details to fall away into the background. At least that's the hope for a whiteboard session in my view.

The idea is simple enough but can be challenging. For myself, I'm a terrible speller and not a great student of grammar. The reason that my editorial shortcomings do not hold me back is simply this: *I don't care to be perfect.* I care about progress and communication more than the judgments that many will place on me or my work, based purely on its form. Further, it is simply a lot easier to draw some labeled boxes connected by lines, than to write a giant document which the team would have to read, review, and criticize, during which I may still be formative in my thinking. This concept is mirrored in the rigorous "design thinking" methodology, where the prototype is simply a drawing.

I strongly advocate that the whiteboard is not a substitute for a solid document based methodology, but only that the document comes later, as required. Referring someone to a document is also one of the lowest common forms of communication. We have likely all experienced the famed RTFM (Read The F-ing Manual!) slough off.

The power of the pen must be shared freely to encourage collaboration and contribution from your team. Assuming a team member is comfortable to take to the board, we must also encourage a culture where these sessions don't become lectures. This is, of course, fine during your college calculus lecture, but if you are aiming to create a dialogue with your peers to explore a complex topic, you will want everyone to feel comfortable and supported enough to contribute.

In agile development, the scrum team naturally convenes around a shared screen, a burndown-based project plan, and hopefully a whiteboard. This methodology favors action, account-ability, and daily progress. When the meeting starts with everyone standing up, the team looks at the stories (work product) that were to be completed the previous day, the plan for today, and the expectations for tomorrow. This communication method leads to very direct and unambiguous exchanges, and thus the helpful nature of the pen.

As companies consider the many challenges and projects involved in their digital transformation, a good-old whiteboard can go a long way. Even for a company with well-established processes, the practice of reviewing those processes and interactions in a simple graphical manner can often bear a lot of great results. You may find out that the documented process is not being followed, were you to put a user and IT designer in the same session. You may find out that there is a missing or duplicative process, or you may just confirm what everyone knows and what is working. Regardless, the activity of having this approach as a core part of the transformative culture will undoubtedly bring value.

A few years ago, in one of my roles as CTO, I worked at a company that had fully embraced the idea of open and free collaboration, based on shared spaces with whiteboards and pens. There were some rules of etiquette of course but among the many positive attributes of the company was simply the work environment. The office had wall-to-wall painted whiteboards, and the teams possessed the freedom to use them. The entire company, from marketing to finance, had adopted this approach of communications and had enshrined some pictures in more complete imagery, while others were more working-level. As I mentioned, the technologist and artist share many common attributes in my experience: the need to communicate and the need for freedom to express their abstract ideas is chief among those similarities.

In sharp contrast, many companies I have worked with relied on an internal method of *push* communications: elaborate presentations and documents that take forever to write—but are never clear enough—are nonetheless written and shared. The problem is that these documents, while useful records of decisions, are really not the best medium for creating a collaborative, agile, and co-creation culture. Finally, once the documents are written, massive email threads are launched to discuss all the needed changes. This is likely the most inefficient manner to communicate. Think about how many emails you receive where the context is not well understood by all parties, and thus the back and forth in a thread is tiring and unproductive. As shocking as this may sound too, a conversation, a call, or a whiteboard are still the best tools available to drive collaborations and communications.

Close your laptop, stop texting or sharing in the Slack channel, and go talk to your colleagues. You will be amazed to find out how much more rewarding and productive the experience is for all participants.

9

STRESS TESTING THE PRINCIPLES

We hope that at this point in our discussion you are beginning to visualize how you might apply our agile leadership principles into your leadership modus operandi. Like any system implementation, we expect that before you attempt to "go live" with what we've prescribed, that you will want to first know:

(A) For what use cases will these principles be a critical success factor
(B) Where they have been applied in the real world
(C) That they are futureproofed

We will address (A) and (B) in Chapter 10, while in this chapter we will attempt to "stress test" our principles by way of applying them to a practical example.

In the software development world, any new application will undergo a stress test before it can be released into the production environment and marketplace. Since end-users will operate the software in disparate and nuanced computing environments, and for purposes not envisioned by the developers sitting in their labs, stress testing places the system into extreme situations, so as to expose any faults or flaws hidden within the potentially millions of lines of coded logic. For our undaunted leadership principles, we propose to test the extremes of organizational entropy.

THE DOOMSDAY SCENARIO

Organizational entropy also draws on the principles of thermodynamics as a way to measure how orderly or chaotic a particular organization might function. In essence, simple business processes find a way, over time, to become more and more complex and chaotic, in the way a block of ice left in the sun will melt away and evaporate into the ether. The entropy of an organization naturally devolves over time from highly ordered to more chaotic. It's why most organizations require periodic resetting/restructuring. Fast-growth organizations that require rapid, flexible decision-making fall prey to hierarchical disarray, as maturation requires more purpose-built, risk management structures. And we have all successfully adapted leadership styles to manage those organizations—form follows function.

But what happens in the fully digital era, where organizations as we know it might include managing artificial intelligence or robotic resources? Or market uncertainties and internet connectivity evolution replace the practice of dedicated resources (employees) with a crowdsourced marketplace. What would leadership look like in a world without org charts? Will our undaunted leadership principles be of value in these scenarios? Are they futureproofed?

Rather than attempting to divine the organization's requirements of the next generation of egalitarian and organic organization structures, perhaps we can stress a more familiar, contemporary scenario, sufficient to fast-fail our proposed leadership style, transformation office remit, and informed visioning methodology.

Imagine that you had a great weekend with your family, basking in the glow of the time spent together, some nice meals, a few errands, card games, and Netflix. Sunday was like most, busy, but perhaps as the day became evening, a little distracted while your mind started to do its weekly routine of thinking about the work week ahead.

Nothing special was yet planned for Monday, except for the normal cadence of operations reviews, action items, follow-ups, scrum team reports and metrics—in short, the usual.

Monday comes, and as you ride up the massive elevator of the Sears Tower (yeah, that's what us hardcore Chicagoans still call it), you see the first meaningful CNN news alert of the day—and that news is not good.

Your company, "ABC Company," has been attempting to diversify your customer base for years, but try as you might, the concentration of sales remains stubbornly held by one major customer, "BigCustCo." Your board is fully aware of this risk but has resisted funding reinvention initiatives and the extension of the products to compensate. Your sales teams have year after year been given strategic targets to diversify the customer base but have been able to make their quotas on the status quo. Bonuses are still being paid for hitting the business-as-usual plan, growth has been modest, and shareholders seem satisfied with predictable revenue streams. This situation has effectively lulled the company into a trough of complacency, dedicating R&D budgets toward placating BigCustCo's incremental needs, while flouting abstruse portfolio innovations.

ABC Company had been contemplating the creation of a digital transformation office, but routinely deferred on such a CIO "indulgence," as the expense for doing so would need to be paid in terms of a budget allocation or an inter-organizational tax on the operating businesses. Rather, the executive leadership team distributes the corporate overhead and the associated tasks of vision setting, strategy, and transformation within the operating business units.

Unfortunately, today is the day your board has feared the most for a long time. CNN has just reported that BigCustCo will be going through a major investigation into financial corruption, their CEO has been fired, and the day-to-day operations have been taken over by a court-appointed executive team who are charted to find the best way to break up, sell off, and exit the business while protecting debtholder and shareholder value the best they can. Effectively, Monday morning has brought you a doomsday scenario.

Your first instinct is to do the rearview mirror analysis. How did we get here? Who was passing the buck on risk management? Why did we fail to execute our diversification strategy? There is no "business as usual" way out of this one. There are no magic bullets or bluebird sales opportunities in the pipeline. Without an immediate, credible, committed resolution plan to address this existential threat, the board will have no choice but to just turn off the lights. The only resources that you have to work with are your dedicated team, who are at the same time completely dumbfounded and desperate to carry on.

What will you do? This situation sounds difficult for sure but has happened many more times than anyone would like to admit. I'll never forget an insufferable travel day, while serving as the CTO of Clear Communications, which ended on the steps of the scandalous Enron, standing there as law enforcement agents chained their doors shut.[26] Our company had been pursuing a sales opportunity with Enron for months and this was the day when we expected to convert the opportunity into a sale. We had done all the analysis, built a demo, and I was there to explain the challenging technical parts to the IT team and the final decision maker. Even though history tends to repeat itself, and the story of Enron is unfortunately not unique, we just didn't see it coming. Had we made the sale and booked the revenue already, the financial hit would have been much, much worse than just opportunity lost.

The most important question here again is simple enough: "What will you do?" No matter what your company chooses, your leadership skills will be tested like never before and will be on full display to every employee. They won't be analyzing action

---

[26] Clear Communications Corporation was eventually renamed Clear and the operation to which we refer is now defunct (not to be confused with any enterprise currently doing business under that name).

plans and debt restructuring approaches; they will be looking for you, *at you*. They will be analyzing your every word, your commitment and consistencies, trying to determine whether they stay and fight alongside you, or head for the door.

What will you do? Will you assemble your leadership team, get a message straight, then call an all-hands meeting to attempt to "calm the team and provide some sense of stability"? Will you reinforce the business as usual?

After you have had the obligatory board call, will you call your team together and decide to treat today like any other and just stall for time while you attempt to come up with a new plan? In other words, will you decide to not trust your team with the brutal truths?

Or will you seize this terrible day to take stock of what your company could be and reimagine the business? Will you decide that the business-as-usual approach will no longer work? The choice now is yours, to either retreat and most likely fail quietly, or to play the cards you have on the table, attempt to pivot your business, and try to "reimagine the art of the possible," based on your market points of view and all the research you have done.

In this scenario, you must consider and face one simple truth: no matter what you say and do in the days following an event like this one, even the most stalwart employees will feel the potential disruption and loss of stability. The result will likely be a tremendous amount of fear, anxiety, and lost productivity, while the new reality sets in. As a result, anything other than authentic, truth-based, undaunted leadership will not be received well. Even if you set aside the ethics of this matter, hiding from, or trying to "manage" the employees, will only serve to give life to the fear and uncertainty you'll need to eliminate. I believe that people have a legitimate right and need to know the facts as best you can provide them; in this way, an employee can decide to join or remain with the company based on what is also best for themselves.

Even if you don't face the degree or severity of the challenge presented in this scenario, a number of smaller disruptions over time may well have the same effect. Let's assume for the remainder of this chapter that with this compelling event as the catalyst, we will reimagine and reinvent our company, starting with the culture, as we rapidly move from complacency to fear, and from fear to growth and reinvention.

The Aristotle Factor

I argue that companies can be far more than a collection of people serving a common set of goals. The whole *can* be much greater than the sum of its parts, as Aristotle at one point conjectured. If we can engage in the process of constant reinvention, intimacy creation with our customers, empowerment of our employees, and real innovation, a company may well serve as the energetic multiplication of all the intentions, goodwill, and thought of the working brains and bodies of the people operating within it. In this way, the company may become powerful, but not arrogant, and the employees may become more engaged in the attainment of the mission, as they will have not only co-created it today but for tomorrow as well.

Imagine what our company would be like if it could become an organization without org charts, levels, and political hierarchies. What if we abandoned the old-school organizational design guidelines in favor of an egalitarian and far more organic structure, focused on collaboration and the full engagement and potential of each of our team members?

As we grow in our careers, we are presented with "the way things are" and the "way things are done." For many companies, the separation between the management track and the technical track may as well be as deep and wide as the Grand Canyon. Managers are groomed to manage as if there is some magic to following protocols and implementing the performance management process. Meanwhile, those who are to be led are considered *resources* and are *the managed*. People are well organized into hierarchical structures where the manager is given charge of a number of resources within their span of control, and so on. Form again follows function.

But what if all this process, structure, and separation between the worker bees and the managers no longer makes sense anymore? If "function" goes out the window, and you're left with a complex organizational form, while all the resources are wondering if their company will remain viable and they will remain employed, you will need to look again at your principles and the motivations of the team if you are to stand a chance of retaining them and the viability of the business. One thing is certain at a time like this: panic and fear will only amplify the risk your business faces, while calm, undaunted, and egalitarian leadership may well right the ship if applied to engage the entire team in the task of doing so.

As for myself, I started off on the technology path with really very little understanding or interest in the "management track." As one assignment begat another and the days became weeks and then years, I started to realize that other people were dictating the projects I was working, their order, their form, and before I knew it, I to had become just a "resource"! I can assure you that this realization met me with a shock and resolve, in that I began to realize that I could be and do more. I could provide more value, and indeed also believed my teams would be more excited, motivated, and understood if I became a leader and took charge of not only the doing of the work but the leading of it. Given I had been well versed in playing the role of an engineer, I had not spent much time worrying about HR, finance, or Gantt planning charts, other than to ensure that my part was done well and on time.

This led me back to higher education for another master's degree, but this time for an MBA. I fully admit that I had no real idea that people did so many diverse and necessary jobs outside of technology development and delivery. As my brilliant business school peers were taking accounting for the nth time, this was my first. They would tease me about my enthusiasm for topics they had so much familiarity with already. I always felt that my complete ignorance was a bit of a gift, as I could just learn without much preconception. In this way, I had classes full of mentors and teachers—until we got to economics: this is where the engineer in me could really shine and do my part to contribute to the collective knowledge of the class.

The professor came in the first night and started talking about the father of modern economics Adam Smith, the invisible hand and all, and ultimately concluded the class by saying: "Now that you all have the history, this really all comes down to the *calculus*, and so the rest of the class will be based on differential and integral equations and their application to economics." Finally! I felt at home with a course topic, but my classmates were all looking a bit peaked now. This was one of my first leadership realizations: that even though we may take different educational and career paths, there are commonalities amongst the "sum of the parts," and the thing that separates us most is merely interest and desire.

My education was eye opening and interesting, but I still struggled with the historically deliberate separation of "interests and desires" between management and the team doing the work.

IN SEARCH OF A NEW MODEL

Given the nature and speed of technology and our working lives, can managers who have no experience or context effectively supervise a team of technologists? Digital transformation requires transformational leadership, and the times of managing such transformation via Gantt charts—just as if it were a project from the 1950's mechanization of a factory—are now passed. I am sure that some managers may well become transformational, but I am even more certain that a new model for transformational leadership is required if they are to do so; thus we argue for the undaunted leadership model herein.

Being "managed," frankly, does not feel very good either. As a leader, our goal needs to be to inspire and empower as a first course of action. The old ways and habits of *directing* and *assigning* are mostly demotivating and may lead to project-oriented progress, but I'm certain that this type of progress will, at best, be merely plotted along the execution path of some management-conceived plan. If we want disproportionate output and change...well, this is the stuff of creativity and passion, not compliance.

Disproportionate output and change are the stuff of creativity and passion, not compliance.

How then, do we create this egalitarian environment, while staying business-plan-predictable in the least? You want to constrain the downside risk of project noncompletion, while allowing for, and encouraging, the upside explosive creativity and passion of your team. If constraining the downside risk of failure may sound like a bit of a counter, "fail-fast" culture, well, it is! In my experience, most businesses don't have either the luxury or patience for failure. Many leaders in place today were raised taking the industrial version of the Hippocratic Oath ("do no harm"), and simply will not tolerate any significant risk.

So how do we absorb failure and iterate on tasks, while we constrain the risk? The approach that has worked best for me is to execute the outside-in process called out in Chapters 4 & 5. There is also real wisdom in breaking the execution down into small iterations that bring value to lead customers. In doing so, we are able to prove to the business that our transformation is having a positive effect and is being well received by our lead customers, and hopefully, as a result, our financial performance as well. It has often been said, and is true in my experience, that "time kills," meaning if your transformation does not return real results within the quarter, half, or year...the project will likely be killed.

In the case of ABC, a quick way to jump-start the recovery could simply be to canvass the adjacent markets for problems in common with BigCustCo, but with some likely nuances. If we can find them and engage the team to become empathetic to this new segment quickly, so we may iterate and refine the adjacent market solutions, we may well find an initial way to limit the downside risk of failure of our business as we experiment with ways to grow and diversify.

This was true for the pharmaceutical industry thirty years ago, as they foresaw a symbiotic relationship with biotechnology and opened up strategies and investments accordingly. Sometimes, these sea changes are less obvious. By the 1980s, the telecommunications industry had been connecting people via copper wire for over a century. Often operating as government-owned entities or under right-of-way monopoly protections, revenue growth came from adding new features (e.g., caller ID, call waiting). But the tighter that telephone network operators tried to hold onto their monopoly power, the stronger the calls for deregulation allowing greater competition and innovation. AT&T was broken up via court order, and with it, a shot heard 'round the world as state-run PTTs (national postal, telegraph, and telephone providers) began to privatize.

Newfound competition is a strong market driver, but one that many leaders will try to deflect away under the temporary illusion of market dominance. While not facing a doomsday scenario, the engineers and researchers at Sweden-based networking giant, Ericsson, were feeling the competition for their core wireline switching products, while at the same time taking notice of interest from affluent, but hard-to-serve markets for nascent mobile telephony solutions. It was not just that Ericsson dipped their toes into mobile communications, building the first mobile network in Saudi Arabia in 1981, but the "all or nothing" approach that they took when entering the market.[27] Ericsson could have just sold their state-of-the-art digital switches to a plan-design-build contractor but decided instead they wanted to come out of the gate with an end-to-end system, including cell planning capabilities and base station equipment.

How that strategy came to be is a bit of commercial folklore, likely some blend of the company line that "a decision was taken"

---

[27]   Pontus Staunstrup, "Mobile systems," Ericsson, www.ericsson.com/en/about-us/history/products/mobile-telephony/mobile-systems

at the corporate level, and the internal research community's bravado that a mobile telephony system was constructed at the working level amongst technologists across a close ecosystem of providers. How the decision was made may be less important than the culture of the company that allowed it to happen—by the time that a strategy was documented to shift into mobile communications, a full product was already developed and proven. Ericsson was, and is to this day, known for its incredible investment, year after year, in research and development. R&D prowess raised the bar across the enterprise for high performance and the confidence to enter any market, knowing they have the ability to overcome any technology challenge.

Of primary importance, then, is that your team is built with high performers who not only understand the need for what you're doing, but they have the passion and will to take action. They need to have the facts, they need to know that you are all-in, and they need to see how they will be rewarded for delivering. This is not a time and place for complacency or bogus platitudes. This is a culture of information, action, accountability, teamwork, high performance, and fun.

Yeah, I said *fun*. When I am having fun, I am far more productive and creative. When I have had jobs where I was essentially plowing my way through someone else's project plan on which I had been assigned a set of tasks, where I didn't really know the reason for doing them, and had no real incentive except for my three percent yearly increase if I played my cards right...I was successful and got the job done, but narrow in my contribution. This limitation came from the management hierarchy and processes of the business's normal operations and the fundamental culture.

Too Many Lines of Code!

As I have mentioned, my first employer was AT&T Bell Labs. They really knew how to start a new employee off successfully if you were willing to do as you were asked: do the reading—lots of reading—meetings with your mentor, participating in design reviews, then taking on the "bug fixing" tasks assigned.

Bug fixing is actually a fairly difficult assignment on complex systems. You first need to really read and understand the written complaint and the intended requirements. If you don't have enough information, then you need to find the person who made the complaint initially and commiserate with them, ask them questions, and learn what the situation was in the environment where the issue arose. Were they in the lab? Were they in the field in a live deployment? Was the problem repetitive or happened once in a while? And so on.

We need to remember the *science*
in our computer science.

Given that computer scientists are meant to be *scientists,* you now need to be able to reproduce the problem such that when you have found a solution, you can test that in fact your solution removed or solved the indicated problem and mitigated the complaint. Amazingly, this is an area of some long-term frustration for me as a leader of software developers. We need to remember the *science* in our computer science. and we must be able to speak in concrete terms and back up our assertions with proof. At times, I have found myself saying that "we need more science in our computer science," to a junior team. It's about fact-based scientific methods. (As you may have noticed in my storytelling, Bell Labs has a way of sticking with you even if you have left a long time ago.)

Now, armed with the full understanding of the complaint and the ability to reproduce it in a similar circumstance, you're ready to hypothesize a solution, or you may be able to just fix the problem straight away, test it, and submit.

Initially, I spent many hours doing all the reading and preparations, and I always asked for a bug report to look at, so that I could have a concrete grounding for what I would be asked to do. I asked to join senior developers during their lab time, and I asked to sit in on whiteboard discussions of problem reviews and new feature development. In other words, I was eager to get to work, always building my knowledge and skills as quickly as I could.

Within a few months of joining, I was being assigned bugs to fix myself. The standard was something like: "A developer can effectively fix one bug every four to six weeks while producing up to ten lines of code per day." This was an all-in number and encompassed every step, including test and submission. It did not take too long until this pace felt very slow to me. I was going to work at the natural pace of the problems, complexity, and availability of time and resources. I was not going to work toward any arbitrary metric. Eventually, my pace was close to a bug a week with as many lines of code as it took.

I recall one weekly meeting with my boss where he shared with me that I was "working too fast," and that my quality must be substandard as a result. I was truly shocked by this statement and assertion. So, I blurted out before I could think "what are my quality metrics?" The answer was that I had not introduced even one new bug since I started working. This is not bragging, but I share to illustrate the acceptable norms. Further, I was informed that some of my peers were also upset as I was not adhering to the norms of the process. I vividly remember telling him "Bell Labs was paying me well for my time, so shouldn't I work as hard and fast as I could?" The answer was to move me onto more advanced design projects, and these jobs took up the full time assigned for sure, as the 5ESS was a complex beast of a product.

These were the days of design, and not experimentation. They were also the days when telecommunications competition was very limited, and the services were fairly rudimentary by today's standards. The Labs had performed statistically significant studies on the causes of software defects, they had built elaborate processes to avoid the occurrence and reoccurrence of bugs, and they had moved to the Deming quality model. The job was becoming more about the process than the work itself. *Process is great and important, but process is not the purpose of an activity, it is simply a method by which you have agreed to carry it out.*

Time to market, speed of development, velocity, and the minimal viable product were still just totally unrelatable concepts. We all had time to do the job right. Right, accurate, performant, optimized, or perfect was just more valued than quick and dirty.

Running with Scissors

Contrast that traditional "process comes first" approach with today's Continuous Integration and Continuous Deployment model of contemporary software enterprises. Whereas pushing code rapidly into production in my early days at Bell Labs would have been seen as the development equivalent of running with scissors, in today's hyper-competitive environment speed to market is king. We accept imperfection so long as there is an upgrade (iteration) coming. This velocity is driven by innovation and by the availability of technology that dramatically enables reuse, almost unlimited supply of high-powered cloud computing resources, and speed. Google is famous for introducing product experiments, testing if they are valued, and if not, killing them quickly (i.e., a market lifespan that can last less than a day).

Times have simply changed, and the digital transformation managers of all enterprises need to be aware that the competitive innovation cycle is short. Followers may follow quickly; experimentation and iteration are key as we may not have enough time to fully study the customers' acceptance or potential use of a product or solution. The rate of change is in fact so high that our customers may not even fully know what they want or need, except in general terms.

The situation that our fictitious ABC Company finds itself in would be far less likely and threatening if they had implemented some version or instance of the Innovation & Transformation Office from Chapter 4. The company would be better aware of the adjacencies and disruptive opportunities in their markets, and hopefully would have invested in forming, debating, and capitalizing on a set of points of view that would have enabled ABC to be more situationally aware and perhaps prepared for this day.

The work would have likewise logically led to the development of a series of innovation projects that could have been shared with and vetted by potential new customers through a market engagement and outreach group, or directly via strategic sales operations. Finally, a business development liaison would have been able to help the sales organization gain an initial new customer or partner traction.

The point here is not to reiterate the form and benefits of having a digital transformation office, but to draw the connection between having such a group and the agility it provides the company in times of market and customer uncertainty. In this way, you may think of the digital transformation office serving the purpose of providing an insurance policy of sorts, as well as its primary purpose to drive the engagement and transformation of the enterprise and its offers, based on an informed and continually refined set of points of view.

MANAGEMENT VERSUS LEADERSHIP

The disciplines of management are valuable. Someone needs to make decisions. No one is arguing that here. It's the protocol rigidity and the pigeonholing/classifying of resources where it all falls apart in my view. We are not resources! We are people, and people are multifaceted. People have many interests and passions and skills. By placing a person into a role and then ranking them against a set of rigid criteria, we are effectively setting the limits of our expectations on them. We are telling them who they are to the organization, what we want from them, how we want it, and we are messaging to them that they need to comply in order to be accepted.

I frequently take a train from my home into Chicago and most days I am greeted by the sounds of a welcoming, but sorely disenfranchised, train conductor. His daily banter, served up in a most-friendly voice, goes something like this: "Good morning riders! You are off today to work, to toil your years away in an effort to please the boss, so that he may make his bonus, while you retain the opportunity to work another day." Or, "Good morning riders! The fat cat bosses will benefit from your work today, as you grind out your lives as a cog in the massive machine of their enterprise." You get the picture.

When I first heard this incantation, I was a bit taken aback. So nicely put, but so sarcastically painful! This person was simply echoing the plight of an individual who had been handled badly in their employment experience and did not buy into the management-speak any longer. He clearly felt like a resource, of no greater or lesser value than any asset the railroad operator employed.

What if instead, we defined people's roles based on their current and aspirational capabilities? For example, I'm a fairly analytical person and consider myself a strong CTO/Architect. I am interested in information technology and how to best apply it to solve complex problems. If I am interested in contributing to the technology selection process in engineering, as I see a particular technology as potentially disruptive, then why would I not just join this working team and participate so long as I can keep my current management commitments? Organizationally, this can come with concerns, fears, and confusion, but I reject the premises on which these reactions are usually founded. This is in fact exactly what I do every day. I find though that the approach can be misunderstood in many of the teams I work with initially. The first concern seems to be "Why is the CTO involved in the selection of a Database?" My answer is simple: (1) It's interesting; (2) I'm interested; and (3) *I can provide value.* None of these factors interfere with my commitment to take on this task alongside my customary responsibilities. Other times, people are concerned that my sitting in might be an expression of my lack of faith in their ability to do the work. This could not be further from the truth. I see this reaction as unfortunately driven by years of traditional management hierarchy practices.

Over time, my interactions with the many teams I have worked with and supported allowed for my extended involvements to be seen as a new normal, with the added benefit of demonstrating my desire to lead from the front lines, from the project rooms, and not from the corner office. I strongly recommend this approach for not only the benefit of the senior leaders, but also so that we create this collaborative cultural element throughout our teams. In doing so firsthand, we will be demonstrating a value we want in our culture—collaboration and flexibility, and the interest in each member of the team to stretch and shape their roles and responsibilities.

Of course, in smaller companies where I have had organizational responsibility for pretty much everything technical, the protocol rigidity was simple to overcome. I just express my wishes for how the organization should behave, I act this way myself day in and day out, and I encourage and reward others for doing so. I believe that in and of itself, this approach has been one of the primary reasons I have been able to join many talented teams as their technology leader while gaining support and acceptance right out of the gate.

If we apply this to a larger organization, like our fictional ABC Company, in the face of their existential threat, one of our first actions could be to have each organization break up into self-directed teams (leaders would be asked to lead via participation instead of assignment), for the purpose of understanding the current situation, brainstorming ideas that each organization, or the company as a whole, could pursue to fill the gap in revenue, or at least buy time until different products or markets could be developed.

To make this effective, we would have to tell our employees the full truth of the situation, and we would have to ask them to do more than what they had been assigned historically. We would have to commit to listen, evaluate, and take action on the ideas that have the best promise to succeed, and we would have to be transparent in our rewards. We would be asking the employees to co-create the short-term and perhaps even long-term company response strategy.

Imagine the engagement and trust that would develop should we take this approach. Our transparency may frighten some employees, and those who were uncomfortable with the new level of risk may well leave the company. They likely would have done so anyway, in my experience, while other employees may see the real opportunity presented by the turmoil, and, as a result, engage at a level they had never done before.

It takes an Undaunted Leader to lead through such a transition, and it takes the persistence to drive cultural change in order to engage the entire company. If rewards are tied to this approach, which I highly advocate they should be, then you may well see the renaissance of your company and its culture. Upheaval may well lead to reformation in a much more dynamic and interesting company format. To top this off, starting every day from a blank sheet of paper could be quite an adrenaline rush (assuming you were able to keep the lights on through the duration).

I am certain that companies today have many great people and pioneering ideas hidden just below the surface of the management structure. Our employees often know a lot more than we give them credit for, and they likely have the keys to growth and recovery in the case of ABC, lacking only the organizational means to instantiate them.

GET IN THE GAME

While a "manager" manages the spreadsheets and processes, a coach aims to pass skills on to a player so they may do their job best, and hopefully in a more fulfilling manner. In business, a "player/coach" is a common way of expressing a "get in the game" approach, fundamental to implementing the undaunted leadership style: breaking down the management rigidity and embracing the unique skills and opportunities presented by the team. A player/coach is, in my view, a reflection of those who see themselves as equal to the team, are extremely interested and engaged in the work of the team, and leads from the perspective of their own participation more than an imposed authority. Clear lines of authority are required and are more efficient but leading by authority should be your last resort and held for only the most rudimentary or dire circumstances. Someone needs to authorize the spending of the budget, and the leader has the ultimate responsibility for the employment decisions concerning the people—but both of these extremes should fall to the background of the day-to-day work and should be fully acknowledged, but not the focus.

Thinking like a player/coach will diffuse any micro-manager tendencies or attempts to do everyone's job for them. The value in this model of leadership comes from authentic leadership and engagement. It's not about telling. It's about listening and co-creating the future for the team and the company. It's about empathy, passion, and doing.

Many have written about the perils of the leader who takes the entire company on their own shoulders. In other words, the leader who attempts to play every role, and by doing so disenfranchises the team! Some organizational analysts have derided the concept of a player/coach as unproductive, as they can neither play their position well, whilst trying to also coach the whole team in action, nor coach well when they see the field from only a single-player perspective. These are not what we are contemplating or advocating here. We may express the player/coach model as part of our undaunted leadership because we are in the game, yet not playing every part. Have you ever seen children play soccer? It's a mess with everyone running to the ball. This is not the model for success we are seeking. Alternatively, have you ever seen a basketball game where the coach is sitting on a chair the entire time, scribbling plays on a small whiteboard, while they randomly scream some incoherent admonishment or player name, like anyone listens to an outsider whose lack of engagement expresses their complete separation from the outcome of the challenge?

Player/coaches are living and dying with the team, while they recognize their role and value in this team is to lead, mentor, and bring the best out of every player! And yeah, sometimes the coach can make a few high-value technical plays themselves because they have "been there and done that" many, many times!

---

*The focus is on the work of making our company
a great provider of value to our customers and an
exciting and engaging place to work for our people!*

In the case of the ABC Company, imagine the leaders as player/coaches leading through direct participation in the departmental working groups, searching for the keys to their response, and ultimately pivoting from dependence on BigCustCo. Imagine yourself in these sessions: how would you approach this conversation? As for myself, I could see this play out very organically as follows:

"Team, we all know by now, and have likely thought about the effect the scandal and dissolution of BigCustCo may have on our company. This is a serious disruption that we had known was possible, but we were not as prepared as we could have been. While there are reasons for this, the time now is not for looking back and pointing a finger or making excuses. We, the leadership team, recognize that this news is potentially upsetting and of great concern to our entire company. We feel this angst, too, but are resolute in the idea that we are a capable team with outstanding people. We have some assets that are ours uniquely and are inherently valuable. We have decided to take this threat and translate it into the opportunity to reimagine our company in a more sustainable, valuable, and high-growth fashion. As we stand here in front of you, we can't say that we know precisely how to do this, but we believe that together, with your commitment, we will have a fighting chance at success. These sessions are our first approach to engage us all in the conversation about who we are today and who we want to be tomorrow as an enterprise."

Then the speeches stop, the facilitation starts, and as the ideas are coming, they are written on the whiteboard for consideration. Perhaps at the end of these sessions, small teams are quickly formed to create an innovation candidate for the top common ideas, and so the process of reinvention will have begun.

The Undaunted Leader—bereft of ego, knows that the answers exist, and assured of principles over destinations—recognizes they must tap into the player/coach as a highly effective model for this environment. If you try to manage the team by hiding the truth, you are done. End of experiment. They will smell it and you will no longer have the sense of job security as an inducement against the management "happy talk." If you try to just tell them what to do, you will most certainly not be able to generate the volume or quality of ideas in an executive conference room without the engagement of the team.

The bottom line is this: player/coaches are loved because they engage sincerely, openly, and transparently regardless of the circumstance. This example of ABC Company may seem extreme, but try applying any other model of leadership and see if you think it holds water.

Common Principles = Common Culture

Living the principles from Chapter 3 is, in my view, the best way to start to truly shift the culture of your business. "Do as I say not as I do" never works. It just places all the responsibility on the person demanding compliance, while leaving the subject of the commands unengaged and disenfranchised. The leader is under constant scrutiny by the team in good times and in bad. The words we say are important, but more so the actions we take and the behaviors we exhibit. My goal is not to reiterate the principles here, but to highlight the importance of their realization in your leadership style as your company faces its more digital and transformed future. It is extremely difficult to change or adopt a leadership style unless through intention. Unfortunately, we humans seem to be able to pick up bad habits more readily than good ones.

So, if we expect to change the culture of our teams or our company, this transformation needs to start from deep within. It needs to start with our acceptance that we don't know everything we need to know already and that the collective contributions, wisdom, and passion of our teams are the strongest asset any company has. We are tasked as the leader to bring this amazing energy out of our teams and into its fullest realization.

Leadership teams and their chosen consultants have a tendency to write down, to document, our core values and mission statement, hang it on the walls, ask our employees what it means in meetings, and have quarterly recognitions for those who express our values. These are not inherently bad things, but if you are not living these values, and if these values are not only understood but accepted and embraced by the teams, then they are nothing more than corporate mumbo-jumbo and will only serve as the measure against which your true behavior will be judged.

Common principles are not only for leaders. Common principles are meant to be *common*, to be *commonplace*. In this way, we want our employees to be on this journey with us as we transform our business. We want their faith, optimism, intention, commitment, and attention. To gain these most valuable assets, they must know that the expectations on them are the same as you have for yourself.

In the case of ABC Company, can you imagine how rapidly unproductive the brainstorming sessions would be if the manager sat at the head of the table, told the team everything is fine, and then started calling the roll of the team for their one good idea? This meeting would be a total waste of time and serve only to further alienate the team.

I once attended an all-hands meeting at one of my employers where the leader gave his spiel each month, followed by the obligatory question and answer period from the employees. In this company, the employees were largely afraid of this leader, as he had proven to be very volatile and at times outright angry and irrational. Over time, the team had learned to not ask questions for fear of embarrassment or reprisal. In frustration, the leader announced at one meeting: "The next time we gather, each of you needs to have one question written down and in your hand. When I call on you, you must read your question aloud. If you don't have a piece of paper in your hand, you will not be admitted to the next meeting." Can you imagine how nervous the team felt? Do you think these were quality questions? For weeks, employees talked quietly about what they may ask that could be acceptable, but not controversial. What a waste of energy and goodwill. I, too, pondered what I may ask as my question. My top choice was: "Is a coerced question worth answering?" Of course, I realize how completely politically incorrect that question was, but it welled up in me like a resistance movement to the theater of the absurd that was playing out on this corporate stage. Fortunately, I was not called upon, and I had elected a less philosophical question by the time of the next meeting, but my feelings followed me around, nonetheless.

You cannot administer or preach your way to create loyalty and dedication, you have to earn it through your commitment, principles, and actions every day! Only through transparency and honesty will the farcical label of "resources" be overcome by empowered teams.

If you accept the need to move to a more player/coach model for your leadership style, then the employees may well also become your teammates. Teammates in the truest sense of the word: your team *and* your "mates." And you may well begin to see them as such, and they may begin seeing you as such. This is the beginning of the wanted transformation of your culture.

Teammates have roles to play, but they also have skill sets that are larger than is required to fulfill those assigned roles. Teammates learn from one another and have common expectations of one another. This is exactly the push-pull we need in order to drive our cultural transformation. Whereas a player may play for their coach, themselves, or their alma mater, a team plays for each other. This culture of a common commitment to a clearly defined and worthy common goal serves to form the bond that unites talented individuals into world-class teams—teams that excel because they help one another freely and, in doing so, propel one another to succeed.

Belief in a Common Vision: Giving Rise to Motivation and Purpose

How do great leaders attract great people to join them in pursuit of their vision? The most powerful reason is simple: when the vision is shared. A shared vision is constructed not only out of the ideas of some visionary but more the collective ideas of the team. Sure, the visionary and/or leader needs to lead. They need to have a point of view and they need to be able to articulate it, and, of course, the company must see a legitimate chance for economic gain from delivering on it. This is all true, but many companies who have lost their vision can still set reasonable business objectives, and depending on their circumstance, may be successful in their own right. What we are going for here is altogether different. With digital transformation, we are aiming for something much greater, for some explosive, self-multiplying rate of change in innovation and transformation.

To climb to these heights, we need every member of our team to be contributing beyond our habitually limited expectations of them.

To climb to these heights, we need every member of our team to be contributing beyond our habitually limited expectations of them. We need their hearts, head, and hands. If they can see the future we see, and if they can contribute to jointly shape it, then we may truly engage and empower our teams to greatness.

If they see that they are rewarded for their contributions and that the culture of the team is one where the best want to be, then they may rise to the level of our transformative hopes and shared expectations. These expectations have no limits, as the team will form and adjust and push and pull one another toward a joint future. Toward their shared vision. The linkage between rewards and contributions is critical, and this too must be transparent. I can assure you that the best people in the world are for the most part aiming for an opportunity for real wealth creation, just like their C-level executive team. They deserve this opportunity just the same.

Too many companies provide little to no distribution of the equity to the broader team and reserve it only for the C-suite. Maybe they get offered a 401(k)-stock purchase matching if they're lucky. Although there is an expectation of disproportionate compensation, tight-fisting the equity will only serve to limit the commitment of the team as they will not have the same type of incentives as the leadership. No one is promoting a model of peanut-butter-spreading equity. But sharing in a common reward only serves to further cement the common bonds and alignment throughout the organization. The work and outcomes determine the value and opportunity for real economic growth for the team.

Just being on the team sets the expectation that high value and contribution is expected and that this team is working toward a mutual goal which, if achieved, will yield a mutual benefit for all. In this environment and culture, the leader must ensure that each team member is contributing to driving the common achievement of the joint vision. If a person is chronically failing to contribute at the level expected, then they must be removed. It's as simple as that. If the team sees that there is any measure of value other than that of the full contribution and passion of each member, they will quickly lose faith in the fairness of their leader. *Fairness comes from consistent evenhandedness in all interactions, and this is a base expectation of talented people,* especially when we are asking them to undertake massive challenges like those presented by digital transformation.

As for myself, I have had the absolute honor to work with and lead many high-performance teams. The people on these teams remain in my circle of colleagues for years, and the reason this is so is due to the fact that the best want to work with the best.

This is not a boast, and the circle is open to all who come, bring their best, and deliver.

One of the most memorable compliments I ever received from one of my colleagues who has worked with me many times was this: "I enjoy working with you because it is always *with you* [not *for you*], and you have always treated us all fairly." That is the reflection of this chapter, as channeled through a great team member, colleague, and friend. Just a perfect sentiment of my desires as an Undaunted Leader.

Our hope here is to challenge and encourage you to consider substituting the old model of management and to instead bravely work to transform the culture of your team by establishing an egalitarian, fact-based, open, engaged, and team-led model, and as a result, fully engage and empower your teams to embrace your digital transformation.

10

CASE STUDIES

B y now, hopefully, you've been inspired by at least some approach, concept, or praxis from our work and are considering putting it to test in your organization. But you may be asking yourself where to start. Where could you apply these principles to aid your team as you progress your digital transformation forward?

One size rarely fits all situations, and we are certainly not professing in these case studies that they will fully conform to the challenges faced by your organization. Instead, our hope is to provide some context and situational (hard-earned) experience, where we applied the principles in this book as practitioners. From this context, you may see where the principles, processes, and structures would make sense to try to implement, or you may at least use them as a starting point for the creation of your own unique response to the specific transformational challenges facing your company.

As Peter and I have spent the vast majority of our professional careers working in the high-tech industry, we recognize that our experiences are shaped and influenced by the nature of the businesses in which we have worked. We hope that regardless of the industry you find yourself serving, you may see the threads of similarity to be able to incorporate what you have obtained here.

We argue this: that all companies—yes, we mean the complete use of the word all—are impacted and will be pressured to transform in some way today and going forward. *Digital transformation is a journey and applies to all travelers.* If you're a third-generation, family-owned, local bakeshop, you likely will need to source your supplies online, accept Apple Pay, and sell your specialty goods via the Amazon Marketplace in order to sustain your cash flow. If you're running a large, brand-name enterprise, you likely recognize that scale does not always win, and that competition is now all around you by niche players brought together in a global marketplace of goods and services. How you decide to leverage your assets, perhaps embracing greater agility while continuing to serve your customers, will make all the difference to your long-term survival and hopefully continued growth in a renewed marketplace.

So why would the lessons learned by a couple of technology leaders apply to you? Our answer is fairly straightforward: the technology of the Internet and soon-to-come AI and Edge Cloud came from our high-tech world, but are now available to you, as they are to anyone looking to execute on ambitious strategies. Further, the perimeter around your business, the proverbial "walled garden," has vanished with the click of a mouse, by a yet-to-be-known competitor who may have studied your business as a basis to disrupt you and start their own.

This technology comes with great promise and opportunity to accelerate your business, but also with a great need to understand how to lead your teams through this time of disruption, brought on by this era of global digital transformation.

We offer you now a few case studies—places where our approach has been successfully applied to an organization under pressure—which resulted in outcomes beyond the expectation of management and staff alike:

- **Case #1: Bending the Growth Curve**

- **Case #2: The Disruptor Model**

- **Case #3: Breaking the Culture of Monopoly Lost**

Our intent here is to offer a window into how you might apply our experience to your next big technology, business model, or market challenge as you transform.

BENDING THE GROWTH CURVE

Challenge: turning up the investment heat on the core technology through an undervalued and underappreciated technology organization

Solution: created a vision for the technology evolution and the technology organization's role and value-add

Result: moved the core business system that had been developed over twenty years to the Cloud in just ten months, while retiring a mountain of technical debt, with less than half the allocated budget and forty percent of the time expected, thus enabling unlimited top-line growth by removing all scale limitations of the core business offer

Our first case study starts with an analysis of an established, private company focused on IoT and analytics applications to enable retailers to maximize sales conversion, through a greater understanding of customer traffic patterns, staffing, and responsiveness, and store layout, display, and sales performance benchmarks. The company had a highly successful flagship service offer, operated as an "as-a-service," delivering to over 1,000 store brands per day.

The company had gained initial success but was now struggling to grow beyond its current scale, due to limitations and technical debt accumulated against the platform technology. (Technical debt refers to the many technical items that did not make it onto the investment prioritization list, and thus remain unresolved for some time.) Based on the wealth of data, experience, and customer incumbency, the company had embarked on a product growth strategy focused on the introduction of business analytics and big data applications, incorporating the existing store traffic solution along with additional data sets encompassing national weather data, government census data, and market data. The board of directors recognized the impedance to growth posed by such an amount of technical debt, but with an impressive value proposition and ROI for the end customer believed that if they invested in the business's core technology, they could "break-out" and unleash significant additional demand for the core solution, while growing the big data analytics product to a level of significant contribution to the company's revenue profile.

The board had allocated a significant budget to reinvent its growth platform but had not been able to establish a plan of execution or priorities. Instead, they had decided to hire a new CTO (*me*) to develop, plan, and lead the transformation of the technology and the technology organization.

I spent my first several weeks as CTO meeting with every employee in the technology organization, key clients, and internal stakeholders across product management, the executive team and board, finance, sales, marketing, and operations. What I found was a degree of diversity of opinion that was just mind blowing:

o Our customers felt they their expectations were met but expressed concerns over the speed of new feature introductions and integration with their IT environment

o My technology organization seemed to know the problems at hand, but without a strategy or prioritizations, were mired in complexity and putting out daily IT fires

o Product management had previously fought for and won a split of the technology group to ensure they had the resources they needed to meet their new product introduction timelines, whilst creating tension within the technology team between the innovation and maintenance camps

o The sales team expressed constant angst over the perceived lack of new capabilities to offer their clients and the pace of the implementation of customer-specific requests o My leadership peers and the board of directors were highly skeptical that a technology team struggling to meet the day-to-day requirements of the company could execute on such a highly ambitious growth strategy

In general, the culture of the company was based in fear—drained by the internal conflict and the walled communications between organizations that had devolved into fiefdoms, scarred from the battles that came before my time. My initial situational assessment: the technology needed investment, the culture needed enrichment, the value propositions were all good, but the time-to-market needed significant improvement.

Forming a Point of View

Clearly, the technology implementation needed improvement and had been underinvested for quite some time. Technical debt was high, yes, but the value of the solution was equally high, and customers depended upon it every day to drive their retail operations. We had some time to fix the situation, as our current value proposition was at least *sticky*, as they say. The technology and operations teams were very much responsible for the favorable customer impression, as they had been managing the current systems with very limited downtime. All this being true, the competition was gaining traction, as they were simply perceived as being more innovative. None of the competitors had proven their scalability, but their story was "the incumbent is slow and old school." Unfortunately, the assessment was partially true. We were a bit slow—there were systemic reasons for our issues—but our internal issues and challenges were of *zero* interest to our customers.

With agreement internally on my situational assessment, I could focus our discussions on a path forward—from the current backlog of requirements, to the process of building the software and for operating it, and to what we wanted to become.

Everything was on the table, and we allowed ourselves to ask the *what-if's* that had not been available in the past. What if we were able to eliminate all of our scale limitations, and we, therefore, grew the customer base by fifty percent a year? What if our competitors were able to catch up before we were able to roll out new innovations? What if, based on our growth, we leveraged the current and growing customer data set to predict behavior versus just reporting it?

With these seeds, we could think through what we would have to do to address the potential futures we were considering.

The vision for the company remained very much the same: we aimed to provide operationally relevant information to enable retailers to better operate their business while maximizing their commercial opportunity. This meant more and better traffic management, better analytics and big data solutions, and more insights into real customer behaviors and shopping patterns and preferences. The question was *how*.

Our point of view coalesced around the notion that the business requirements were generally correct, and the purpose of the solution was clear. The operational environment for the solution had become outdated, and the implementation of the technology had become far too complex, due to years of add-ons without a clear architectural governance. The result is what I like to call the *Christmas Tree* approach to software development: any time you find a shiny new requirement (ornament), implement it (hang it) on the existing system for all to admire.

The problem is that at some point, you can no longer hang new ornaments without making a mess of things. This had been essentially what had happened over the years. This was also due to a very short term and tactical approach to the investment plan for the technology organization. The budget only permitted the addition of small capabilities year over year; the team had never been given the opportunity to simplify, refine, or refactor the implementation.

We decided that we needed to resolve the operating environment issues as a direct and critical step to unleash the growth potential of the company. We had many conflicting aspirations for the portfolio, but none of them would become available if we did not remove the challenges to the scale of the operations environment itself. We also had a significant list of fairly high priority technology issues to resolve related to technology obsolescence, security, and the concurrent development of our growth portfolio in analytics.

Creating a Plan for Success

To inform and direct our execution plan, we next had to start to form a point of view on the technology options and opportunities. We then scanned the market for potential options and solutions for our operating environment challenge, and after looking at the tremendous growth and maturation of cloud computing platforms and providers, we decided that we would migrate our solution to the cloud. This was our initial technology point of view.

Cloud computing was driven by the need for highly scalable, flexible, and ubiquitous computing environments from every technology-driven market segment today. Banking had moved to the cloud, and automotive, health care, and a significant proportion of retail had all moved to cloud-based offers. If we adopted a cloud-based approach, it would be disruptive to our implementation, but enable unlimited growth and market access. Thus, the *Get to the Cloud* project was born out of this point of view and a joint understanding of the technology team.

After an extensive evaluation of cloud providers—no small task—the team was able to create and articulate the beginning of an approach, and *plan* for the *Break Out*: (1) we would move to the Cloud in a "lift and shift" manner, so as to not impact the existing quality or operations of any customers; (2) we would also remain fully available for new customer acquisition and growth during the migration; and (3) we would continue to invest in our growth portfolio. Our vision was to reinvent the business solution while continuously operating it.

We constructed a series of internal presentations to share our approach, objectives, timeline, and budgetary needs. Given the apprehension about technology promises in the organization, I took great care to construct our story. Years prior, an admired colleague had coined the phrase "Horsey Piggy Ducky" for the level of language that technologists needed to develop or adopt to be understood by the more traditional business function leaders. Us techies and geeks love acronyms, and just can't help but to get drawn into talking about all the depths and nuances of technology.

Once leadership gave their approval, we started communicating technology overviews, innovation updates, and progress updates regularly with the rest of the company during our monthly all-hands meetings. We needed the company to understand the technology organization more fully, and the critical role we all had in moving the business toward our joint vision. And the technology organization needed to feel understood and valued.

Work the Plan

In order to pull off such a transformation, we had to work our plan every day. We built a migration plan for moving our business to the Cloud, and a set of supporting agile sprint plans for the software, hardware, and firmware changes that would be required to accomplish the overall project. We also outlined a set of clear measures and timelines. We did *not* go about writing detailed design and functional descriptions. In other words, we did not revert to strict waterfall project management but instead added metrics and measures to track our progress and give us an early indication if we were on plan or off. All this, too, helped the team and company recognize that their contributions mattered and were in service to drive the desired outcome for us all.

Week to week and month to month, we focused on the plan, the challenges, the execution, and our end goal, and were able to accomplish a full migration of a twenty-year-old system to the Cloud, without an outage, in ten months. We also retired a mountain of technical debt and introduced many key new capabilities and brought on new customers as we progressed. We did this all with less than half the allocated budget and with forty percent of the expected time.

The key word in this story is *we*. True to the Undaunted Leader principles, I was in the fight, shoulder to shoulder with my team. I spent countless hours with the team discussing the challenges of the day, what we learned in the last sprint or deployment, what the progress metrics looked like, and what we would try next to overcome the challenges we faced. We faced issues with technologies, Cloud environments, and yes, legal sword rattling from vendors struggling with what our transformation meant for them, all of which made us stronger and more focused and more cohesive. I had many hard decisions to make, and some of them I had to make alone; those were and are the exception. This does not mean consensus leadership, instead, this approach favors progress over perfection and collaboration over control.

Favor progress over perfection and
collaboration over control.

When I had to make unilateral decisions, or even had to let a few people go, the team knew that this was done in the best interest of the whole, and not from my pride or ego. Teams are made of human beings, with remarkable histories and experiences, that when applied as individuals are limited to the impact we can make. But when great people come together with their full intention and collective desire to succeed, being committed to a point of view, a common vision, and a plan to execute…well… magic happens, and an ethos of innovation and accountability emerge as the culture of the day.

The Disruptor Model

Challenge: take market share by direct competition with the incumbent, legacy vendors with established, demonstrable products

Solution: invoking humility—actively listening to the customer; facing up to the brutal truths about the portfolio; recognizing that we don't know what we don't know

Result: broke from the mediocrity of continuous refinement; took advantage of the incumbent arrogance, while changing the economics

While market leaders lead, their rival competitors compete. This was the case with an upstart telecom software vendor founded and headquartered in a lovely city in England. The company, like many of its type, had started out simply enough: it was a collection of close friends and colleagues performing services projects one at a time. The company suffered from the classical boom and bust of project-driven businesses. When a new project was won, the entire company focused on that particular design and delivery, to the exclusion of everything else. Over time, they started to see a repeat problem common amongst all their communications service provider clients: their operations support systems were simply outmoded for the challenges of the (then) modern communications networks.

It became apparent that a services-led business model was not fully producing robust enough solutions to meet their clients' present and future needs. So, over time, the company made a concerted effort to develop a hardened, flagship product, embarking on the difficult journey from services provider to a product-driven business model. Adding burden to that transformation was that now, with a product focus, the company had to migrate its technology to the cutting edge of cloud computing, virtualization, open source, and the like.

Fortunately, the market competitive culture of this company meant that everyone embraced the strategy and was up for the task. Everything about this company screamed egalitarianism and meritocracy. We were all in this together, and we all expected the best for and of one another. We reviewed each other's work, we worked together, we socialized together when we could, and we became a close-knit, us-against-the-world, high-performance team, companywide.

In this type of environment, you don't have to *demand* anything from anyone. The team knows who is doing what and who is really putting in their best effort; the team knows if someone is slacking and the professional coaching comes from peers as well as leaders.

While everyone understood the end goal—what success looked like—that path to get there was not actually all that clear. My research group was tasked with a simple enough objective: Innovate! But what did that mean exactly, they wondered. It sounded simple enough, but in order to innovate, you first must have an appreciation for your present circumstances, access to those who represent the group for whom you aim to innovate, a set of guiding principles that codify your point of view, and very talented thought leaders/technologists to help do the difficult work ahead. Oh yeah, and you also need to really understand the problems your innovations are aimed to address. The *why*, as it were.

Our transformation would need to enable us to disrupt the sleepy Operations Support Systems marketplace by reinventing and reimagining the applications required to enable the communications service providers to grow and operate their businesses. Our *why* was to innovate or die.

The Mindset of a Disruptor

Disruptors wake up every morning with a vision in mind for how they might grow and bring value to their customers. They see themselves as outsiders and underdogs. They study the problems and the discontinuities in their industry and explore them with customers in open conversations about what the future could look like. They do not lead with a product, because most times they do not have one built yet. They lead with empathy and understanding. They are flexible and agile and quickly adapt to the customer's needs. They do have a point of view and a set of core beliefs that they share within their companies, but they see them as a work in progress. Their brand is thought leadership and innovation driven. They have nothing to lose and everything to lose.

Disruptors have nothing to lose
and everything to lose.

The disruptor has many flaws and weaknesses too, for example: "They have no experience"... "They have no scale"..."They sound good but where are the customer references?" These and many more are all good and reasonable arguments the incumbent may make against them—they know this, and they don't care!

While disruptors may be maverick, they are not typically cavalier. With a lack of any incumbency, they have to leave their egos at the doorstep, as we discussed in Chapter 2. I recall one of many long days/nights out with a colleague while we worked to pursue a very large customer opportunity. The customer contact was effectively the head of the network planning group for a very large international internet and business services provider. Our company had invented a very novel and innovative approach (for which I was a co-author on the patent) to change the network planning process into a more ongoing and evolutionary one. So, the customer posed a complex question about the nature of the Internet itself and framed it in the fashion of a test: "Does the Internet possess deterministic characteristics, and thus is it fair to plan my network on this assumption?" Something like that.

Turns out, rather than hand waving this question, we felt that a deep, thoughtful assessment was required to lend as much concern to the person asking it. The answer required a significant consideration of the customer's context or connectivity to the Internet and a consideration of their technology choices. Furthermore, once answered, it may be best expressed in a complex formula of probabilities. Being the disruptors that we were, we dropped everything we were working on, and a few of us, including a great mathematician colleague and I, spent several days doing this assessment. We studied their networks and created a position on the matter, with the purpose of modeling this question in a piece of software we would implement for our customer.

I presented our view, our thoughts on how to really frame the questions, our view on their process for network planning, our technology and patented approach that may incorporate this concept, and then finally...wait for it...the *math* that proved our point.

After all of this complex work, the interest of the customer, pride in our approach...well...I half-expected a round of applause once the formulas hit the projector screen! Instead, I was faced with the stark reality that the crowd was not all on the same level of understanding, and many were a bit lost.

After swallowing my pride, I ended up learning a bit more about a potential customer, and they came away with the impressions we aimed to leave—we did not have a product and they knew it, but they also knew that we clearly understood the matters at hand and could credibly create the optimal solution. Through our passion, our point of view, and our willingness to do the work to earn the business, we overcame all the anticipated objections that a "challenger" would face.

Many times customers will buy from a disruptor based on the unique set of skills, thought leadership, and the passion they may bring. The process of being tested too allows them to sharpen their value propositions and search for additional market inefficiencies to disrupt.

The act of disrupting an established market, with numerous barriers to entry and scale, is an exercise in humility. Disruptors are students of the market Goliaths, and they will even appreciate an incumbent for its longevity and market prowess—but watch out, as that admiration will be short-lived once they have identified their proverbial stone-and-sling with which to topple a Goliath.

Points of View – Keep Iterating

You probably realize by now that we strongly advocate for challenging and improving your points of view. That is really the *work* we must do to understand the market and our customers. So much stems from this simple concept!

It is critically important though to be open to challenging your point of view. As long as we are living the leadership principles, we should be able to be intellectually honest with one another, even if this honesty may challenge our core point of view or innovation. No company has the *right* to exist! Companies exist because they create and deliver value in the eyes of the market and their customers.

The initial inventors at our disruptor enterprise had formed a point of view that data and process integrity could really only be maintained if data were acted upon *in-process*, versus post-process. This is a very strong concept and it has many merits. The downside only comes when the data already exists and was created by another system. If a new system was to be built from the ground up, we had a significant technology advantage. But if our scope of work was to replace an existing system, then the rigidity of the model and approach had some downside as well.

As we grew in scale and became more successful, we were always able to deal with the data migration issues, but it became increasingly clear that the core belief around systems and data integrity was too limiting in some instances. We needed to challenge and potentially *disrupt ourselves*, and after some very thoughtful and often heated debate, we did just that. We created additional capabilities that allowed for less-constrained uses of the database while holding the data integrity in the best form for the more structured usage.

I have worked at several other companies that simply could not reimagine themselves as anything but what they had been, instead of what the market was telling them they needed to become. As we have said before: "Disrupt yourself or expect to be disrupted!"

When a core understanding or learning no longer fits the market or customers you serve, this is the time to channel your principles and understand what is really needed. This is the time to empathize with your customer again, and it's time to keep a clear view of the competitors and what they may be doing or saying. In my experience, this humility and openness make all the difference in maintaining a competitive advantage in times of technology and market disruption. This does not mean that you should abandon your points of view and research, or that you necessarily were "wrong" before. The technology industry changes rapidly, and software innovation and application have no market segment boundaries.

A digital transformation of a competitor may well be motivated by their desire to completely disrupt their industry or your business or just themselves, or how they can utilize technology to operate more efficiently or interact with their customers. Regardless of the motivation, the only constant is change, and the rate of change is on the rise. Analysts point to the turnover of the S&P 500 as a yardstick for digital disruption: *Forbes* reported that the average tenure of companies on the S&P 500 will shrink from twenty-four years in 2016 to just twelve years by 2027; at that rate of change, about half of the S&P 500 companies will be replaced in the next ten years.[28]

Some of that disruption will come from a form of the inspired, isolated invention that results in what economists might call creative destruction. This type of disruption is really hard, if not impossible, to predict or manage. Many companies start off with a grand, brand-new idea only to fail in either execution, vision, or grounded points of view on their markets. But for those small set of companies who find a vein of gold in the bedrock of the business world, they may find success if they can capitalize on

---

[28] Bob Davis, "Digital Transformation Was Already Important, But Now It's Also Urgent," *Forbes*, February 19, 2019, www.forbes.com/sites/forbes-techcouncil/2019/02/19/digital-transformation-is-already-important-but-now-its-also-urgent/?sh=6c650709422c

their claim. If not, some other company will surely find a way; this is just the nature of innovation itself.

Companies in this category may not even know or care that they are disrupting an ecosystem or competitive landscape. They just have a good idea and are pursuing it. You may not identify them before they identify you as a competitor. Regardless, they likely have some innovative angle or technology, so once you see them, take them seriously. There probably will not be an analyst report that shows the total addressable market this company is going after, and there may be no big splashy marketing blitz— these companies and disruptors are like pebbles tossed in the ocean that one day may cause a tidal wave. They come from obscurity and launch entire new categories of offers and value. Good examples here would be Apple or Microsoft in their early days.

Find a Way to Change the Economics of Value Creation

I am particularly mindful of the disruptor category of strategic "followers," who exist to exploit the weaknesses of the incumbents within a market. In many ways, these businesses are some of the most dangerous, as they study market forces and competition diligently, acutely aware of exposed inefficiencies and unmet needs. These companies aim to minimize their market risk: by following, not ground-breaking, they may look for a set of players already making money in a market as their reality check against self-delusion.

There are no constraints or limitations on disruption. A new entrant could actually *make free* what the incumbent provides as a scarce resource. This may sound difficult, but in fact, has proven to be fairly successful in technology-driven markets. For example:

o Google disrupted the paid navigation business by making maps free in return for monetizing your location with targeted advertising o An open source company upends conventional, licensed software vendors, giving commoditized applications away for free, and selling maintenance contracts instead

o Online banking takes advantage of lower fixed asset and operations costs, offering attractive fee-free services that can entice depositors to finally let go of the security blanket of branch banking

This free-for-all (pun intended) model is based solely on the discontinuity of the market. A disruptive competitor may have practically zero operational costs when it can operate solely in the Cloud and online, while the brick and mortar incumbent has market share, but a higher cost of operations that cannot compete in a like-for-like model with the upstart. This is clearly a cry for self-disruption and reinvention.

This type of disruption comes not necessarily from a competitor driving a wedge into your market, but more from a technology innovation that simply reduces the value of the incumbent's business. For example, the providers of relational database technology have been significantly impacted by the availability of an open source alternative named MySQL. A license that previously cost thousands, if not millions, of dollars now may be downloaded for free and supported via an inexpensive support company. What should the incumbent do in this case? They have a heritage business, it's becoming less viable every day, and they have a choice: should they hold on tight to their legacy value proposition and fight the customers' migrations to the alternative technology, or should they disrupt themselves, acknowledging this pivot in their industry and provide value-added applications that further their value creation and contribution, while allowing their core product to take its natural path? There are no easy, formulaic answers to these questions, but they must be asked and answered in some manner. **The worst strategy is simply to do nothing and let the market and others determine the fate of your value proposition.**

Breaking the Culture of Monopoly Power Lost

Challenge: break the culture of legacy leader complacency, before revenue declines and lack of growth gravely diminishes the value of the business

Solution: created an irrefutable body of outside-in thinking and forecast; drove business and portfolio innovation and planning through purposeful collaboration

Result: attracted a strategic buyer for the business, under the cloud of a cash shortfall and the calls from industry pundits for a piecemeal sale

Our last story involves a historic, highly respected telecommunications engineering services and software organization. This company was one of those organizations that you never heard of, but that impacted your daily life, responsible for architecting the high-reliability local phone network in the United States. They invented and patented many of the acronyms in telecom for networking protocols and management, and they determined the technical requirements for much of the equipment that would be purchased by the phone companies and how such components should be deployed to work together effectively and safely. These were *the engineers' engineers* to the communications service providers. They were the experts.

And many of the people who worked there knew it.

For many decades, much of the innovation in the phone network came from within the halls and conference rooms inside this organization. Mass market ideation: an oligopoly of service provides pushing new offerings universally to every subscriber. Caller ID, Call Waiting, and other features weren't requested by phone company subscribers (they wouldn't think to ask or even know how to), but subscribers were happy to have them when rolled out.

Such purpose-built, inside-out thinking prevailed for years until the Telecommunications Reform Act of 1996 (TRA). TRA allowed anyone to enter the public-utility-protected communications business, and let any communications business, including the then Baby Bell companies, compete in any market. Instead of sharing innovation across the national network providers, the phone companies had to compete on services and performance, and likewise, the engineering services vendors would have to create their own vision for the future of competitive networking and the roadmaps of offerings to support a consumer base that would now have choices in the marketplace.

Keep Buying or Start Saying Your Goodbyes

Breaking out of the comfort zone of a monopoly mindset was easier said than done. As defenders of what they had helped to create, the most reliable telephone infrastructure in the world, our engineers' engineers were not going to let something as arbitrary as a government-imposed industry structure stand in the way of their life's work. And, in the process of clinging on they began to pretty much anger every one of their customers trying to reinvent themselves:

- o Network equipment providers were forced to conduct expensive pre-sales testing to make sure that their new products would work with the embedded support systems that ran the network operations—testing that would be conducted by those that wrote the standards, of course, in a highly-protested and captive market

- o System integrators were hamstrung from building business-level solutions for telecom when faced with software engineers who refused to share their closed, monolithic, proprietary architectures and data models

- o Industry analysts and reporters who criticized the legacy of difficult-to-maintain "spaghetti code" were punished with a withdrawal of press access and interviews

o Non-traditional, competitive service providers—wireless, cable companies, international players—were subjected at the beginning of every sales pitch to an obligatory PowerPoint slide education on the storied Bell history before any presentation of challenges or solutions were discussed

o The legacy Bell network clients, whose pleas to move decades-old systems off of expensive mainframes, were met time and again with business cases where the migration costs outweighed the next generation systemization benefits

That insulated business model worked until it didn't. The telecom broadband recession of 2000 hit everyone hard, and new levels of efficiency needed to be considered so that the industry could get back on solid ground. New communications services required a next generation of software systems so that service providers could integrate voice with surging data and video services. While legacy software and services providers kept pitching their high-reliability value propositions, upstart software vendors were focused on *time-to-market* for innovations as a differentiator for telecom service providers trying to compete for subscribers.

Slow to respond to its newfound competition, our engineers' engineers were forced to move from *build* it to *buy* it, and went on a bit of an M&A spree, which those inside and outside the company knew had become a survival strategy: *keep buying or start saying your goodbyes.* As in our first case study, integrations of architectures and cultures were difficult. The "next-generation" business unit was given the mandate to essentially cannibalize the legacy systems core business, which was itself trying to find ways to support new services and slow the half-life rate of revenue decline. The hub of invention had quickly lost its industry dominance, as evidenced by its sales and product management talent defections. Over the years that followed, ownership changed, leadership changed, and it became easier and easier to find a parking space in the headquarters parking lot.

A Return to Growth

What we witnessed may have been the fine line between pride and arrogance. Pride is powerful. It runs deep and stands tall against adversity. It's very personal and walking that line in business can be a disconcerting venture. People have strong views, based on their experience and learning, and at this organization, every step the company was taking was wrought with opposing views, both internally and externally.

Decisions that were once rooted in math and science, were now made, under hyper-competitive pressures, by gut feelings standing on pillars of pride. Upon joining the leadership team of this organization, I quickly realized that I needed to turn the management of this business back into a fact-based environment: decisions based on facts. If you want to make an argument based on the facts, that's great. I'm fine with that. Then pride will allow you to see yourself in strategies that you can get behind and drive into the organization.

Decisions that were once rooted in math and science, were now made by gut feelings standing on pillars of pride.

We had to rebuild the portfolio and the innovation process to prove to the market that we could reinvent ourselves, and was worthy of a prospective buyer (our then-owners strategy for their buyout). I had to find a common denominator, a common language that would get our business line units on the same page, and on the same page with customers. I also wanted to change the way we approached our customers, from "We are the market leaders and we're here to take your order," to "We want to talk about your business."

What we could all agree on, and what became our new science, if you will, were the key business processes that underpinned our customers' operations. Given our legacy in telecom, our researchers, software engineers, integrators, and even salespeople were well versed in how service providers operated—how networks were engineered, how the equipment was inventoried and provisioned, how orders were taken and customers billed, and how service troubles were identified and repaired. We could then do what we do best: work with our customers to identify potential problems and solve them. We could map out each process, step by step *with them*, and look to see where the pain points would be and where we could offer a solution. Any gaps would be addressed by our product innovation roadmaps, and/or, in a novel approach for our organization, we could find partners to help us solve them where we could not alone. And we could quantifiably measure our improvements in operator efficiency and time-to-market, instead of boasting abstractly about technology hype cycles and adoption rates.

In doing so, in listening more and soapboxing less, we actually began to change the relationship with our customers. They began to refer to us as *partners*, not vendors. For years, we had tried to throw the term partner around in our marketing-speak, but it fell to the floor when delivered with the arrogance that made the term ring hollow. But now, with a shared fate—with our survival in the balance—our innovation would be centered on our customers' business, not our fascination with technology.

We were now selling suites of products across a business process. And our customers were reinforcing that message. That notoriety got us noticed by the marquee players in our industry, who now saw the potential to make a broad, end-to-end impact on their customers' operations. At the eleventh hour, in what seemed like we had used up the last dollar of cash, we were purchased by a strategic buyer, and global networking giant, where perhaps the next chapter of engineering *for* engineers could continue.

11

THE LEADERSHIP MOSAIC

When we set out to write this book, we did so because we firmly believe that there is a need now for a renaissance in leadership, especially given the do-or-die challenges presented by digital transformation. We believe that digital transformation requires a clear vision for everyone to contribute to and follow, inspired by an informed point of view, delivered through a humble and authentic leadership style, resulting in innovations that are valued by dynamic and changing markets. We also believe that the wonderful people that you work with are not inspired by business plans or performance reviews—they choose to leave or stay because of **you**.

We know that change is hard, yes, but asking you to reflect upon and change some of your fundamental leadership principles won't just happen magically from reading a book. Such fundamental change must come from deep within, and it must be genuine. What do we mean by genuine, you may ask? Here are a couple of experiments to try in your personal life, in order to reflect on what the word *principles* actually means:

o If you own a watch of some sort (a wearable steps counter or an old-school wristwatch perhaps), take it off the wrist that you normally wear it on and put it on your opposite wrist. Just for a week. That watch that you have worn for twenty years on your left wrist will feel a little uncomfortable on your right. You'll notice it every time you pick up a pen or take a sip of coffee. That's change. That's taking notice of change.

o Sit down with your child, or a trusted friend, look them in the eyes, and tell them that you have decided that for the sake of your relationship, that you would like to become more "transparent" with them. A transparent parent. See how that goes.

o Listen to a new genre of music—*we strongly recommend jazz*—for a week. Jazz, and only jazz.

Why jazz? Because Wynton Marsalis, legendary trumpeter, composer, and instructor, once opined in an interview that while science suggests that the only constant is change, jazz is *how we experience that change.*[29] In his book, *Moving to Higher Ground: How Jazz Can Change Your Life*, Marsalis explains a musician's relationship to their principles, helping them with:

1. *Adjusting to changes without losing your equilibrium;*

2. *Mastering moments of crisis with clear thinking;*

3. *Living in the moment and accepting reality, instead of trying to force everyone to do things your way;*

4. *Concentrating on a collective goal, even when your conception of the collective doesn't dominate;*

5. *Knowing how and when to expend your individual energy.*[30]

---

[29] Talk of the Nation (audio interview), *Wynton Marsalis Moves Jazz To 'Higher Ground'*, NPR, September 2, 2008, www.npr.org/templates/story/story.php?storyId=94198246

[30] Wynton Marsalis, *Moving to Higher Ground: How Jazz Can Change Your Life* (New York, Random House, 2008)

As you enjoy your week-of-jazz experiment, try to observe the journey these artists take within a piece of music and reflect on the journey that has been your leadership experience. A jazz artist will search deep for a unique starting place, and then just launch themselves into the unknown. Although it may seem disorienting at times, the beauty is in the journey—an authentic journey that requires the transparency to expose their inner feelings and desire to share their vision with the listener.

To illustrate the point, I recommend listening to "Jazz at the Pawnshop," recorded by Gert Palmcrantz at the Stampen in the Old Town section of Stockholm in 1976. While dubbed the "best jazz recording of the century," what stands out for me were all the background noises recorded: the tableside conversations, the clanking of cutlery, and the banter between the musicians were all part of the session. As the story goes, Palmcrantz just set up some microphones and the band started playing. No mic checks. No tweaking dials and adjusting gain. Just a principled journey of pure musicality and co-creation.

Okay, while we think everyone should at least have some appreciation for jazz, we're not about to turn this book into a *La La Land* homage of some sort. We mean only to say that we are not prescribing a leadership blueprint: you must adapt to your style, to your strategic goals and challenges. We want you to think more abstractly about your leadership style. We want to encourage you to reflect on the "shape" of your style—the *mosaic* that you are assembling, and the emotional response that you are trying to create with your colleagues, in the way a jazz artist tries to connect, rather than just *play*. Leadership, like art, is a constant experimentation and evolution—a perpetually unfinished work.

My appreciation for abstraction comes again from the art world. Artists have a natural proclivity for stepping back from the noise and reflecting on life, love, and humanity. I try as well… when I can. Our lives as leaders are busy and hurried. Deadlines come and go, and expectations are always high and ever-escalating.

It's often challenging to find a rhythm to your life that enables you to live it, and not just get through it. "Tomorrow's another day." For me, a reprieve at an art museum in the middle of a busy travel week forces me to take the time to wander and ponder. It's hard to pass up the fourth customer dinner meeting in a row, but sometimes you have to step away in order to break the cycle of thinking the same thoughts day after day. *Sometimes, you have to choose art!*

On one such occasion, I was speaking at a trade show in The Hague, and in the middle of the frenzy, I snuck out to the Gemeentemuseum Den Haag, a well-renowned contemporary art museum that I was told had some works from the masters: Monet, Degas, and Picasso. As I wandered through the halls of this wonderful building, I came across a collection from Piet Mondrian (1872-1944), a Dutch painter and theoretician whose works became very abstract towards the latter part of his life. One piece in particular, which Mondrian named *Victory Boogie-Woogie*, struck me to my core for its abstract ability to say so much, and yet nothing specific at all.

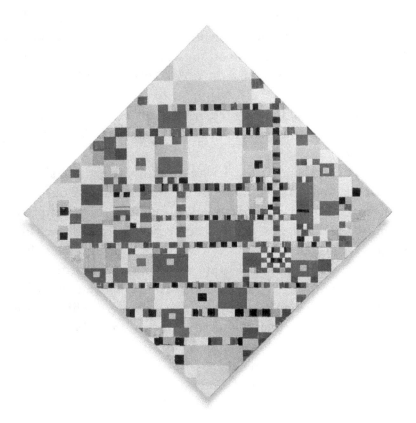

Victory Boogie-Woogie, by Piet Mondrian
©2020Mondrian/Holtzman Trust[31]

I was captivated by its simplicity and intricacy, the color and the balance, the chaos and the order...all his experience and passion and artistry (including his love of jazz), absorbed onto this canvas. Mondrian evolved this style, dubbed Neo-plasticism, as a response to the horrific chaos of World War I. Mondrian sought to use the transformative nature of art to bring harmony to society through geometric shapes and primary colors. These things were clear and representational, though we may see them

---

[31]   With express gratitude to the Mondrian/Holtzman Trust for permission to include Victory Boogie-Woogie

as abstract. Mondrian's partner in the Neo-plasticism movement, Theo van Doesburg, once described the grounding nature of the style: "We speak of concrete and not abstract painting because nothing is more concrete, more real than a line, a color, a surface." While ground-breaking, this transformation was rooted in Mondrian's humility with respect to his craft. He saw his art as merely a channel.

"The position of the artist is humble.
He is essentially a channel."

—*Piet Mondrian*

What has stuck with me the most about the *Victory Boogie-Woogie*, was that this Mondrian was an unfinished piece of art, and yet you may have never noticed that if you had not read the museum exhibit placard. This piece is truly an exercise in *progress over perfection*. Mondrian died in 1944, before completing the work. It was a reflection of his anticipation that the end of yet another World War would this time represent the beginning of a new hope for a new world. While an unfinished work, Mondrian's message still pervades, through his artistic principles, his creativity, and his humility. We, his audience, can fill in the details.

In Mondrian's work, I can see the unfinished mosaic that is my leadership style. We are all unfinished works, and we must humbly seek to discover and project a set of leadership principles from which our audiences can "fill in the details" of the digital transformation vision that we are trying to paint.

Look, *digital transformation can be a downright beast.* I have seen it bring out the best in people and I have seen it bring out their absolute worst. When we aim for consistent principled leadership, we aim to express the best of ourselves consistently, as we and our teams seek to bring order and harmony to the uncertainty and tumult that comes with change.

So, at this point in our final chapter, I am picturing you at your desk, Miles Davis playing in the background, your watch on the wrong wrist, confessing to your teenage daughter that you nearly failed your first semester of college. Brilliant. Now, let's try on some real change. Here's your next challenge: bridge the gap in your organization between your millennials and your giants. You know it exists. You may not want to face it, or you've delegated it, or you're hoping it will resolve itself "at the working level." In the back of your mind, you know full well that such discord represents real economic and opportunity cost.

So, let's address the gap. Head on. Your proof of concept. Abstract the challenge and think through the leadership principles necessary to shape it.

EINSTEIN COULD BE SITTING IN MY CHAIR AND IT WOULD NOT MATTER

I remember the exact day that this thought rushed into my head like a crashing wave on the shores of my self-awareness. It's the realization that experience is not always respected or wanted. Many times, it feels as if gray hair is looked upon as a liability. I took my first technology job while I was still a teen in high school. I did all sorts of electronics technician work for an industrial controls company in my hometown. I soldered circuit boards, made cables, fabricated electrical wiring, laid out circuit boards with tape and transparencies, and developed rudimentary BASIC programs. From those humble beginnings, college followed, my competence grew, and technology continued to advance at an ever-accelerating rate. Initially, I just leveraged existing technology, but very quickly I started contributing my own inventions and advancements to the art of this progress. I like to joke with people today that I have used and forgotten more technologies than many people ever know existed!

Throughout this time, my education continued, while each year of employment was copiously spent solving problems with computing technologies that, at first, fit in rooms, to ones that sat on your desk, and ultimately in your hand and in the Cloud. The amount of change and progress in technology that has so dramatically advanced over that period is just striking as we look back, was impossible to predict, and was hard to grasp while you were in the middle of it all.

Who do we think drove those advancements? The answer is straightforward and right in front of you—the generation of those giants in their field. Some used the technologies of the day as others were inventing them. The pattern persists still today. New engineers and leaders enter the field and create the state of the art, and over time, the next generation becomes the establishment and the cycle continues. My most ardent belief is that the new need not push out the older or more experienced: those who came before and who are still in place have a lot of value to offer. For some, they continue on the pace of technical growth and advancement of their skills, and can make their contributions in an agile scrum, are using Go, Python, Java, and they like to play with hot, new technologies like they always have. Others may become comfortable in a specific technology and continue to support it for a long time. Remember Y2K? Guess what, those systems still exist, and although the world did not end because of the year 2000 date rollover, there was a lot of effort made by a lot of technologists to ensure that the older systems did not fail.

A very common misconception is that when a new technology comes out, it quickly displaces the older generation. This is just not the case. The world and our lives may well be far simpler if this were the case, but it just does not work this way. When a new technology becomes available, the engineers and designers have to face the reality of today's implementation, which is usually the collection of years of effort, development, technology advancement, and adoption. As a result, the new meets the old, but the old has a very long tail of life left in it and the overall environment of a company's IT becomes a bit more complex each step of the way. Sometimes, we have the need or opportunity to retire or replace/refactor the old technology out. This too takes time and care. The technologies of a company are the collective contributions of the engineers who worked to develop them over the life span of operations. As such, those people are just as relevant and valuable as the next generation, and we need to treat them as such. To do otherwise is an all too common mistake of epic proportion.

The technologies of a company are the collective contributions of the engineers who worked to develop them over the life span of operations.

Fast forward to the companies of today and the increasing number of millennial developers. It's easy to open a requisition for a new developer and list all the amazing new technologies of today as requirements. "I need a person with C# skills, .Net, or Java with Kafka…blah blah blah." *What you most likely need is a person who can solve problems by developing technology-based solutions with the toolset your company has chosen.* It should be taken as a given that the individuals considered have the tools-based skills. But experience in solving real problems is truly a key determinant for the success of an engineer. We need a mix of experience and youth to be the most effective, and we need a culture that truly values both. We need to create a culture where we value contribution and competence over anything else.

WHY DID YOU BOTHER TO HIRE ME?

Mary was a Silicon Valley veteran from the days when the focus was actually on the silicon. Mary had amassed a resume from the most notable enterprise computing brands, toiling on the front lines of product and business development. She was an ever-diligent student of her market, a natural strategist who could step back and see the whole competitive chessboard at play, and a master at developing credible and compelling value propositions. Mary was also a great listener, supporting her teammates when they struggled and made sure they felt appreciated for their insights, even when they were overlooked or taken for granted by management.

Mary saw the need for cloud computing long before the days when it became a popular buzzword. Mary also recognized where cloud could play and where it would be met with skepticism. She could pick the winners and losers. She even left Silicon Valley at one point to work with a global software vendor which was very late to the cloud game, but she was marginalized by a win-at-all-cost culture that didn't want to hear her calls for judicious application or targeted solutions. She was particularly ignored when she tried to express the credibility gap that a new entrant in this space would face when butting heads with the established market leaders—those who had defined the space and who had fully stood up their first-mover advantage. When you're fifteenth to market, she thought, some level of humility was warranted and understood. No such luck here.

So, after banging her head against the wall for a while, Mary went back to Silicon Valley. This time she was fortunate enough to work for a market leader. Fortunate to work for an innovator whose brand was synonymous with customer experience. Fortunate to be asked to join a business development organization where all her experience would be brought to bear to help their customers support their most massive digital transformation programs. Fortunate. Or so she thought.

To her bewilderment, what Mary found instead was a similar compartmentalization of her experience as she had faced with the legacy provider, but this time not from complacent leadership, but from her own peers, her teammates. It was subtle, at first. Her memos on market segmentation or solution architecture ideas were not read (she assumed as much as she did not get any feedback on her communications). She was asked to participate in every customer meeting but noticed she wasn't included in the impromptu meetings at her office. She would get awkward stares from conference rooms she would pass by, where some of her project team was gathered.

Over time, it started to become more obvious that the folks in the room were all of her millennial colleagues. And the folks left to meet at the coffee station were her baby-boomer peers. But that couldn't be it, could it? That her views on solution architecture were dismissed because of her age? Why, Mary thought, was she hired in the first place? On her next business trip, the answer became clearer: because their customers wanted to see and hear from someone with her experience, with whom they could trust their critical IT functions. Their customers needed her. Her employer needed to put an experienced face on their youth-inspired innovations.

Mary thought about broaching her predicament with management. She thought about how to characterize the cultural gaps in an informed and constructive manner. As a trained strategist, she knew not to present a challenge without having first developed some potential solutions to offer up as part of the discussion. She struggled with that a bit, as it seemed like all the answers pointed directly at leadership itself. That's a hard sell, as she had seen time and time again with stubborn customers. But she knew that she had to try. She knew that this type of sub-optimization had economic consequences. She couldn't quantify them, which would make her pitch less compelling, but at least she had enough data to start the discussion.

That was until Mary came into the office the next morning, only to find her manager now in the conference room, whiteboard marker in hand, leading a millennial-only discussion with the same subset of her project team. Really!? Do they not see the same thing that she was seeing? Or do they not care? Or maybe it was the fact that her boss was himself a millennial, which never mattered to her, at least until that day.

MIND THE GAP

Have you ever flown all night to head to the UK, only to find your way to the Heathrow express train to Paddington Station, and then on to the Tube and a whirlwind of activity? I have spent many weeks doing exactly this. If you ever do or have undertaken this travel turmoil, you will be presented with this simple, elegant, and direct warning painted plainly on the concrete floor in front of you: "Mind the Gap." Simple enough. Don't put your feet or anything else in the gap between the train and the platform. The consequences would be dire if you failed to take this command seriously. There are many such gaps in our working lives. The gap between expectation and reality, the gap in the budget perhaps, and the gap in the available workforce to staff your digital transformation.

Although the unemployment rate is a constantly changing factor of any economy, one thing that seems to never change is the need for talented people, whether technical or not. We have devoted this entire book to the topic of leadership during the times of digital transformation because, in part, of this inescapable truth: skilled people don't come in one package. They are younger. They are older. They come from all walks of life, family histories, schools, and neighborhoods. The reality is that we need them all. Emphasis on the word *skilled* of course. No one is looking to add uninterested or unskilled people to their teams, just to keep everyone busy. No, we want and need the best of the best, knowing full well that this pool of people will have many options to choose from for where to work and devote their energies. Given the flattening of the global talent market, due to the inescapable democratization of the workforce, enabled by the proliferation of internet access and high-speed broadband, we can and need more than ever to attract the best people. They simply can work remotely for almost any company in the world. They have far more choice than ever, as do we.

We need the millennials and we need the giants, and most importantly we need to create a safe and productive culture where both may collaborate and drive the growth of our business and the success of our teams. This need to attract, retain, and harness the collective skills and intentions of the best people is the key difference between a successful digital transformation and a failed one. While we scoffed at whether some companies truly believe this, people *actually are* the most valuable resource any company has. Assuming there is a budget or some mechanism to employ them, the rest is up to the leaders to inspire and grow them in the direction of the objectives of the enterprise.

How do we do this? It won't just happen by itself, that's for sure. I think this comes down to forming the joint vision for the future you are aiming to achieve and then seeking those like-minded people to join your cause. You must aim to build a team of highly motivated superstars who want to make a difference. Those people need to know that making a difference for the company will have the opportunity for making a difference in their lives, too. They need to know that you will ask of them the same that you ask of yourself: commitment, transparency, humility, industriousness, and your full intention to jointly succeed. You want people who want to be their best and give their best, and those people might be wide-eyed college graduates who see nothing but the future. You will also need people that have "been there and done that" before. You will need some experts, some gray hair perhaps, and you will need to crack the code on how to *Mind the Gap* as you span the generations, and how to show your team how to do so as well.

Throw away all your preconceptions and misconceptions and consider the principles we've outlined in this book. Paint your leadership mosaic.

Making Connections

We want to thank you greatly for your attention and commitment. We had something we wanted to share, and we appreciate your desire to join us on this leadership journey that has taken you this far in our book. Our lives are busy, we are overwhelmed by the constant influx of information and interruption, and as a result, we are a less contemplative society. Technology provides many distractions, but hopefully, it will also start to free us from our more mundane tasks and provide us more time to think and reflect on life's biggest challenges, opportunities, and gifts.

The principles in this book are shared, in part, to help you make more meaningful and purposeful connections with those that you work with. Authenticity, trust, honesty, creativity, consistency, positivity, gratitude, vision, and purpose all work together to provide an environment for the success of your business, in order that you may have the best opportunity to grow and thrive. Or for when you have to become that proverbial "*weed*," in order to help you and your team stick it out through a rough patch.

The onslaught of disruption and change in our lives and business have driven many of us to seek real connections in a false environment. Millennials seek community and connection in social media but never find satisfaction there. Giants feel left out by the pace of technology and social change. Friendships cannot be orchestrated, and collaboration cannot be automated. Likewise, many leaders today, under the stresses of digital transformation, are reverting back into a programmatic management style, engrossed in tweaking forecasts and putting out fires, to the point we have lost a thoughtful, iterative, informed process for reinventing our businesses.

If this book makes you feel more reflective and more introspective, then great! We are very, very happy. Share it, discuss it, tear it apart, test it, and hopefully come to your own conclusions about how and where to best apply the thoughts presented herein. We have discussed many concepts, stories, principles, and reflections on leadership. Perhaps our offering has shed some light on the realities, opportunities, and consequences of leadership in both positive settings and more challenging ones. Our goal has not been to criticize for the sake of it. We all have greatness within us, and we all have fallen short of that greatness from time to time. What matters most is that we strive for progress over perfection within ourselves as well as our teams. If we have the humility and authenticity to try, learn, and adjust accordingly, we may begin the journey of changing ourselves, and thus the culture of our teams, and in doing so maximize the opportunity for the success of our digital transformation.

*I have learned so much in the practice
of leading teams and I'm sure that I
have so much more to learn.*

It is often said that success has many fathers, while failure has none. We need to shed this thinking and eliminate it from our company cultures. Failure is an outcome of trying something new and taking a risk. Failure from taking an uninformed risk is usually a disaster waiting to happen. Even if you are informed and have a strategy to succeed, you may fail at times. Your odds will be far better though, should you adopt some version of the process called for herein.

As for digital transformation, the time is now. Transform, or cease to exist. For those who don't dare to act, failure likely will also be at your doorstep soon. Today, you must constantly strive for improvement, agility, and growth. Your competitors will simply pass you by if you choose not to grow and innovate. You have many choices as to how you and your company will undertake this challenge. You can try to set yourself up for achievable success, or you can throw caution to the wind, or hopefully, you will take our advice and form strategic points of view and innovations to capitalize on the opportunities you find, and then act upon them in a principled manner to lead your team to a new level of success.

So, we leave you with this question: Now that you have this perspective, what will you do with it? If you place our book on the shelf and never think about this again, we have failed you and you have wasted your money. On the other hand, if you try the ideas out, adopt some, reject some, come to an approach that works for you...then we have done our job well. The choice is yours. It always is.

Adan K. Pope is a leading authority on digital transformation, strategic technology leadership, and technology disruption, with over thirty years of career experience. Adan has served as a senior executive for many enterprises executing a digital or portfolio transformation that led to their strategic renaissance, growth, and at times, acquisition. He has held almost every role in software technology innovation and development from software developer to chief technology and innovation officer for some of the communications industry's most innovative technology companies. Adan has also held executive leadership roles in companies serving the retail analytics/IoT, gaming, and most recently outsourced marketing services industries, as well as held the chief officer title for innovation, industry architecture, and strategy.

o Chief Technology and Innovation Officer, InnerWorkings

o Chief Information Technology Officer and Chief Strategy Officer, Ciena Blue Planet

o Chief Technology Officer, ShopperTrak

o Vice President of Technology and CTO, Ericsson Support Solutions Business Unit

o Chief Technology Officer and Chief Strategy Officer, Telcordia Technologies

o Head of Planning Systems Business Unit, Amdocs

o Head of Research, Cramer Systems

o Chief Technology Officer and Vice President of Engineering, Clear Communications

Adan has collaborated and spoken extensively on the opportunities, emerging technologies, standards, and patterns for the reimagination of the communications industry while co-authoring several patents in the process. He holds a Master of Science in Computer Science and a Master of Business Administration from

North Central College in Naperville, Illinois, and a Bachelor of Science from DeVry Institute of Technology in Columbus, Ohio.

Peter Buonfiglio is an expert business strategist having worked extensively in information and communications technology organizations. He has amassed a far-reaching career experience in helping high-performing enterprises extract the most value from their brand, portfolio, and channels. Peter cut his teeth in market research and management consulting, which piqued his interest in organizations that were struggling to differentiate or that had lost their way. He later stepped into leadership roles that spanned from large, complex engineering organizations to startup entrepreneurial teams.

o Strategic Marketing Director, Ericsson

o Strategy & Business Intelligence Director, Telcordia Technologies

o Vice President of Sales & Marketing, Fralo Plastech Manufacturing

o Vice President of Marketing, Rsoft Design Group

o Head of Network Integrity Practice, Bellcore

o Global Research Director, Electronic Data Systems Management Consulting Services

Peter was graduated from Harvard University with a Bachelor of Arts in Economics. He was certified in Driving Strategic Impact from Columbia Business School.

Adan and Peter are also the Co-Founders of Taraxa Labs LLC. Taraxa was created to provide a safe space for leadership from private enterprise, public sector, and non-profit organizations to let their guard down, get out of their comfort zones, and to challenge the status quo. Taraxa Labs recognizes that the digital transformation game is filled with imprecision, moving targets, competing interests, security threats, and the inevitable, sometimes inexplicable, setbacks and failures that must be mitigated with a strong vision and informed judgments affecting organizations, technology, and people. Its mission is to offer leadership a sandbox for reimagination and reinvention while providing the practical tools and guidebooks to help navigate your transformation journey.

CPSIA information can be obtained
at www.ICGtesting.com
Printed in the USA
FSHW020644160121
77663FS